MIDDLE MANAGERS AS AGENTS OF COLLABORATION

Paul Williams

T0314069

First published in Great Britain in 2019 by

Policy Press
University of Bristol
1-9 Old Park Hill
Bristol
BS2 8BB
UK
t: +44 (0)117 954 5940
pp-info@bristol.ac.uk
www.policypress.co.uk

North America office:
Policy Press
c/o The University of Chicago Press
1427 East 60th Street
Chicago, IL 60637, USA
t: +1 773 702 7700
f: +1 773 702 9756
sales@press.uchicago.edu
www.press.uchicago.edu

© Policy Press 2019

British Library Cataloguing in Publication Data
A catalogue record for this book is available from the British Library.

Library of Congress Cataloging-in-Publication Data
A catalog record for this book has been requested.

ISBN 978-1-4473-4300-4 paperback
ISBN 978-1-4473-4303-5 ePub
ISBN 978-1-4473-4304-2 Mobi
ISBN 978-1-4473-4302-8 ePdf

Cover design by Robin Hawes
Cover image: iStock
Printed and bound in Great Britain by CMP, Poole
Policy Press uses environmentally responsible print partners

Contents

List of figures, tables and boxes

About the author

Dr Paul Williams worked as a public sector manager for over 20 years in Welsh local government, occupying posts in a variety of policy areas including town planning, community development, sustainable development and corporate planning. He then moved into academia where his career encompassed research, teaching and consultancy in public policy and management. He has undertaken a wide selection of research studies at local and national government levels in Wales on topics such as managing equality, sustainable development, community strategies, the role of elected members and working in collaboration. He has a track record of publications, reports and books in these areas and his particular research interests centre on collaboration, especially leadership, learning and knowledge management, integration in health and social care, and the role of individual agents – boundary spanners – in processes of collaboration. He is the author of *Collaboration in Policy and Practice: The Role of Boundary Spanners* and Honorary Associate Professor at the Crawford School of Public Policy at the Australian National University in Canberra.

Acknowledgements

I have been encouraged and sustained throughout my research and writing of this book by my family. My wife Jan has contributed many insights from her long career in public service management and leadership, and has constantly reinforced my contribution to knowledge and understanding in the field of collaboration. I have also been stimulated by the academic excellence of my daughter Sophie who has published a number of articles and her first academic book. My love and thanks to them both and to my son-in-law Darren.

The research for this book would not have been possible but for the time and patience extended to me by countless managers and practitioners in a number of public service agencies across Wales. I am extremely grateful to them all for their valuable reflections and insights into their management practices and collaborative behaviours. I have been fortunate to be associated with the work, knowledge and experiences of a number of inspiring academics, and I am indebted to them all, especially my longstanding friend and collaborator, Professor Helen Sullivan. Lastly, I am very appreciative of the helpful and constructive comments provided by an anonymous reviewer to the first draft of this book.

1

Introduction

No single actor, public or private, has the knowledge
and information required to solve complex, dynamic
and diversified problems; no actor has an overview
sufficient to make the needed instruments effective;
no single actor has sufficient action potential to
dominate unilaterally. (Kooiman, 2000: 142)

Contemporary societies are faced with a seemingly never-
ending torrent of complex, stubborn and sometimes intractable
problems and issues. These are diverse in nature, crossing
time and space – they can be local, national, global or inter-
generational – and their management and resolution challenges
public agencies and governments to the utmost. Climate change,
sustainable development, health inequalities, asylum seekers,
terrorism and crime, poverty and exclusion, poor housing,
unemployment and lack of educational attainment are but a
few of these 'wicked issues' – but they all share a common thread
– they do not respect conventional boundaries of profession,
organisation and governance. Rather, they are entangled in a
complex web of problem definition, causes, solutions, priorities
and resources. What is most important is that it has been the
increasing recognition by policy makers and governments over a
number of years that the management of these types of problems
and issues cannot be resolved by single agencies and actors
operating independently, instead, they demand collaboration
– forms of cooperative behaviour designed to secure the most
effective, efficient and responsive outcomes for service users,
citizens and communities.

The nature and trajectory of this collaborative imperative has been manifested in different ways in the UK and across the world, but there is little doubt that it will continue to shape the character of future public policy and management. Arguably, the enduring 'age of austerity' has placed increased demands upon public authorities to work together towards jointly agreed goals and outcomes. A considerable body of research and experience has been accumulated on the practice of collaboration in public policy. What is particularly apparent from this work is how complex and challenging it is in design and delivery, and most salutary of all, the evidence of its success is far from overwhelming. Researchers and practitioners have invested significant time and resources into endeavouring to understand what makes an effective collaboration – the determinants and factors that combine to deliver agreed upon outcomes. The evidence suggests that these are a complex interplay of both structure and agency, but with considerable debate as to their interaction and precedence. Agency concerns the role, behaviours and decision making of the many actors who perform on the collaborative stage – leaders, managers, practitioners, policy makers, government officials, politicians, representatives from the private and third sectors – all of whom in various ways assemble to deliberate, design and deliver collaborative policies and strategies. The profile and performance of a number of these particular types of actors have attracted significant attention by researchers and academics. Unsurprisingly, there is no shortage of material on leaders and leadership, there is some work on street level practitioners, but with some notable exceptions (Agranoff, 2003; Williams, 2002; and van der Wal, 2017) the spotlight remains comparatively weak on 'middle managers' – and this book aims to address that deficiency. It concerns the role and management of this cadre of manager – 'the middle manager' – operating in spheres of collaboration. What role do they perform, what approach to management do they adopt, what skills do they deploy, how do they behave, what motivates them, and what are the tensions and ambiguities facing them?

This focus on middle managers is considered warranted because of their influence and importance managing both within and between organisations. They occupy a unique position in the bureaucratic hierarchy sandwiched between top management and frontline practitioners and professionals. They mediate and channel communication up and down the organisation, and are linked to other departments through various joint working and inter-departmental arrangements. They are responsible for a prescribed set of functions and duties; they have line management responsibilities for staff; and often manage budgets. Arguably, because of their control of resources and their accountability for performance, they are acutely aware of their status and power. It would appear that if this cadre of manager did not embrace the collaborative imperative, despite the best efforts of leaders and front-line practitioners, the prospects of its success would be compromised. Conversely, a collaborative middle manager offers the potential for more successful outcomes, particularly those that might involve mainstreaming and whole-systems change. There is evidence to suggest that middle managers have been experiencing a number of pressures both in the public and private sectors as a result of organisational changes such as delayering which have called into question their value. References are often made to 'the sticky middle' that accuses middle managers of being resistant to change, and slow and bureaucratic in decision making. Middle managers themselves articulate feelings of being 'squeezed' – between the imperatives of top management, and the realities of operational life from below. In a similar vein, problems of poor performance in organisations sometimes seem to land at the door of the middle manager. Given these perceptions, it may well be that the future careers and direction of effective middle managers might lie in managing outwards through collaboration, rather than upwards and downwards in traditional hierarchies.

Who is a 'middle' manager?

The notion of management is somewhat contested. A distinction is often made between administration and management – the former revolving around the deployment of resources against a backcloth of existing rules and procedures, as opposed to management that implies some discretion in the choice of resources against desired objectives. In reality, managers are often engaged in both to varying degrees. A further complication comes with the distinction made by some between professionals and managers. Here, managers are seen as 'a group of people who are separate from those doing the work' and who have 'some formal authority as well as a set of activities, such as budgeting, performance management, setting up the organisational arrangements, which they perform to direct and control the others' (Flynn, 2002: 4). Again, this dichotomy is not particularly helpful because most managers' career enhancement is through a professional structure. Noordegraaf (2015: 39) suggests that managers are 'the embodiment or personification of organised action' because 'they occupy formal leadership positions' and 'are able to get things done through others'. However, a formal definition is problematic although a differentiation is often made between managers at different levels in an organisation.

There is no consensus over the definition of what constitutes the 'middle', and as Thomas and Linstead (2002) point out, its boundaries can meander over different levels of management, and therefore be contingent on a particular organisational structure; and the functions of middle managers can sometimes be blurred and stretch into those of senior management. The problems of definition are made more problematic by the traditional separation of roles between managers and non-managers being compromised by new working practices such as teamwork, delayering and empowerment strategies, and by the reverence afforded to professionals through their claims to unique knowledge and expertise. Perhaps it is understandable that some middle managers feel threatened, squeezed and fragile in the light of these threats; however, some new forms of movement consider their role to be critical to the transformation of organisations through their leadership and championship of change.

Following this convention, the focus of this book is on 'middle managers' – a group of actors who occupy positions in a tier of management located between frontline practitioners and staff who engage directly in delivering services to customers or support those who do, and a top level of management – directors and executives who have strategic and corporate responsibility for the planning, delivery, governance and performance for their organisation. Middle managers are often defined by their position in the hierarchical chain of command of an organisation – they can head units or sub-divisions; they can have responsibility for specific functions, areas of policy, geographical jurisdictions or statutory duties – they may be involved in the planning and delivery of services directly but also can include support and administrative services such as information technology and legal services. Noordegraaf (2015: 40) differentiates between 'line managers who are responsible for producing things and staff managers who are responsible for making production possible', although in practice these can be combined. Some examples of middle managers from a recent research study in a Welsh local authority (Williams, 2015) include:

Service Manager for Adult Services; Supporting People Manager; Service Manager for Integrated Safeguarding; Service Manager for Commissioning Services; Senior Manager for Conservation and Sustainability; Head of Inclusion; Group Housing Manager; Head of Public Service Support Unit; Sports Development Manager; Principal Planner

and for a Welsh Local NHS Board:

Emergency Planning Manager; Service Development Manager; Community Service Manager for Integrated Learning Disabilities; Integrated Service Manager; Team Manager (District Nursing); Facilities Administration Manager; Service Development Manager.

Clearly, this is a disparate group of middle managers who share some communality but also some differences, and these need to be unpicked in the course of any discussion and analysis. This focus reflects a positional perspective, but there are other ways of categorising managers, for instance by role, by their work and by their activities and behaviours. Van der Wal (2017) refers to three broad types of public manager, other than top manager/ executive – line managers; programme/project managers; and staff managers. However, these are not always mutually exclusive. Middle managers do attract significant sources of power primarily by virtue of their positional status, control over resources and their authority over their subordinates. They develop a set of skills, language and values that reinforces their legitimacy, and manage through the use of a variety of techniques including strategic planning, project management, human resource management and performance management. Middle managers tend to be acutely aware of their internal management responsibilities particularly as a conduit between top-level management and frontline realities and pressures. Middle managers, particularly those with devolved budgetary and performance management responsibilities, demonstrate a significant level of allegiance to their home organisation. This often represents a source of tension when they are engaged in collaboration with other partners – they can suffer most acutely from feelings associated with loss of control, power and autonomy.

Outline and structure

The book opens in Chapter 2 with a consolidated overview and analysis of the diverse and inter-disciplinary theoretical perspectives framing the management practices of middle managers operating in theatres of collaboration primarily involving multi-agency and cross-sector contexts. The intention is to provide a comprehensive synopsis of the state of the art on this topic of study – the models, theories and inter-disciplinary perspectives – drawing on both UK and international literature sources. This chapter provides a critical summary of the main theories of collaboration to provide both macro and micro viewpoints in which to situate the role of agency. The contested structure/agency argument is incorporated into the opening discussion. This review then focuses specifically on the theoretical literature concerning middle management and managers both in a public and private sector context. Mainstream management theories are presented and interrogated to capture their essence, particularly as a benchmark against which notions of collaborative management can be judged and contrasted. Conventional intra-organisational management involves crossing vertical (for example, status, levels of hierarchy, span of control, superior/subordinate) and horizontal (for example, division, site, departmental) boundaries, whereas theories of collaborative management are concerned with organisational, sectoral, cultural and many other boundaries. This review attempts to consolidate perspectives on collaborative management – the management practices and strategies that are involved – connecting, buffering, learning and transforming; and the particular leadership approaches that are deployed, particularly when working in teams and groups. It looks at approaches, styles, skills and competencies but also the challenges, ambiguities and tensions of working in this milieu. Boundary object theory is used to illuminate the barriers to, and conversely the carriers of, effective collaborative management practices. In addition to a public sector focus, private sector theories around alliance management especially in the context of public–private partnerships and strategic alliances are probed to assess their relevance to the overall investigation. Insights into cross-boundary management are presented from the emergent literature on this subject (O'Flynn et al, 2014).

The following three chapters represent the central core of the book, providing an in-depth exposition and analysis of the main components of managing for collaboration by middle managers. They draw on existing material from policy and practice in the UK and internationally, but critically are informed by my own research on collaborative working in Wales, undertaken over the past 15 years. My research and experience has been accumulated through both commissioned research projects on aspects of collaboration, and seminars, workshops and management development programmes with managers from organisations in Wales – primarily public sector agencies but with some involvement from representatives from the private and third sectors. Evidence from this body of research has already been used to support a variety of peer-reviewed publications, but this book also draws on previously unpublished commissioned reports, particularly the following:

Williams, P. (2013) *Integration in Health and Social Care: The Locality Model and the Design and Delivery of Mental Health Services in Cwm Taf LHB* (Unpublished)

Williams, P. (2013) *Managing in Collaboration: A Local Government Perspective* (Unpublished)

Williams, P. (2014) *Working in Partnership: The Police and Crime Commissioners* (Unpublished)

Williams, P. (2017) *An Assessment of Middle Mangers' Approaches to Collaboration in South East Wales* (Unpublished)

It is necessary at the outset to briefly outline the particular institutional and public policy context of Wales in order to better frame and understand the subsequent examination and discussion. Wales is a small country with a population of just over three million primarily concentrated along the coasts of North and South Wales, with a significant number in the valleys of South Wales, and a very large and sparse rural heartland. It suffers from a disproportionate share of social, economic and environmental problems manifested in disadvantaged and impoverished communities particularly in the former areas of manufacturing and mineral extraction; health inequalities; low standards of educational attainment; rural poverty; and long-term unemployment. The architecture of the arrangements for its governance consists of:

- Devolved Welsh Government since 1998 but with very limited tax and law-making powers; an annual block grant from the UK treasury (£16 billion for 2017–18) to allocate on a wide range of public services with the major exceptions of defence, policing and social security that are not devolved matters. The trajectory of devolution is constantly being re-assessed and scrutinised particularly in relation to the annual financial settlement and greater law and tax making powers.
- 22 all-purpose local authorities across Wales are responsible for the design and delivery of a wide range of local services covering housing, social care, environmental health, education, planning, transportation, leisure services and waste disposal.
- Seven Local Health Boards are charged with the planning, commissioning and delivery of all health services.
- Four Police Forces cover Wales but policing is not a devolved function but rather, an integral part of an England and Wales structure.

- A range of non-elected and regulatory bodies covering diverse policy areas in culture, sport and the environment, and operating primarily at a national level, further contributes to the institutional architecture of Wales.

Since devolution in 1998, a feature of the public policy landscape has been the frequent re-configuration and re-organisation of public services driven by attempts to resolve boundary issues between agencies and professionals, improve coordination, provide greater policy coherence and promote efficiency and effectiveness between agencies. The thrust of these changes has been structural rather than agential in character with a condition that might be described as 'strategic incontinence' or a proliferation of strategic intents, characterising most policy areas, and arguably a frustration with the ineffectiveness of policy implementation on the ground. Boundary issues appear to bedevil the policy scene despite constant attempts to resolve or ameliorate them, raising the perennial question of the efficacy of structural solutions to tackle cross-boundary issues.

This organisational turmoil is characteristic of the approach to health services over the last 15 years, and a particular problem relates to the lack of integration between health and social care – the latter being the responsibility of individual local councils. The organisation of local government has also been a fertile area for change, and a review of local government (Welsh Government, 2014) again has proposed a significant reduction in the number of local authorities, although the recommendations have not been universally welcomed and not implemented. Rather, some interests have viewed more collaboration between councils as the best way forward as opposed to further structural rationalisation and upheaval. The Welsh government has consistently espoused collaboration, or 'partnership working' as its preferred terminology, as an integral component of its policymaking paradigm (Welsh Government, 2004; and Simpson Review, 2011). This has been promoted through legislation, statutory duties, funding initiatives and numerous strategies across all policy areas and levels of governance. However, this profusion of strategies continues to cause problems relating to lack of coherence, poor integration and ineffective coordination with a consequent loss in efficiency and effectiveness particularly at a local implementation level. Various plan and partnership rationalisation programmes have attempted to resolve these issues, and collaborative inter-organisational arrangements based on the footprint of local councils such as Local Service Boards and its successor Public Service Boards have attempted to provide strategic direction and joint working. These Boards are made up of representatives from local councils, Local Health Boards, the Police, the Fire Service and other interests particularly from the third sector. In addition to these 22 Public Service Boards, partly because there are probably too many and inappropriate mechanisms for all public service issues, the Welsh government has also promoted a regional dimension to collaboration (Welsh Government, 2013). This manifests itself in various permutations of cooperating adjoining local authorities working together in areas such as the frail elderly, children's adoption, youth offending, trading standards, safeguarding children and family support services.

The reality or threat of frequent organisational and structural fluctuations presents a problem for managers and others charged with designing and delivering public services. Apart from the destabilisation and uncertainties that characterise major change processes that can often be tortuous and prolonged, re-organisations often undermine working relationships and networks between middle managers painstakingly crafted over many years. Perversely, many are not evidence-based but rather a product of political whims and current fashions. In addition, structural changes are not always accompanied by a commensurate investment in the capacities and capabilities of those managers who are expected to work in the emerging new organisational environments.

The prevailing Welsh public policy context provides middle managers with a range of structural enablers and barriers in which to manage collaboration. The foremost of these are described as follows.

1. A variety of legal powers have been placed on some public agencies – notably, local authorities, Local Health Boards and Police authorities – to work in partnership with each

other on various common interests – particularly in the context of Public Service Boards. However, this duty can be interpreted to various degrees because of the lack of specificity inherent in the notion of 'partnership' or 'cooperation'. The imposition of collaboration is sometimes counterproductive, particularly if it is not accompanied by other essential preconditions of engagement.

2. The configuration of public sector organisational boundaries lack coherence and coterminosity in a number of policy areas.

3. Accountability and governance arrangements are materially different throughout the institutional landscape – organisations are held to account through democratically elected local authorities; appointed public bodies such as the Local Health Boards; democratically elected Police and Crime Commissioners; management boards and committees of third sector organisations; and private companies' Boards of Management – different rules, different constituencies, different ethical standards and codes of conduct and different accountabilities. The extent to which a common 'public service standard and value system' can prevail is highly problematic.

4. Performance management systems and auditing frameworks are diverse – some agencies have responsibilities linked to the Welsh government; some, such as the Police, are linked to the UK government; legal and statutory duties are prescribed for many, and various Audit and Ombudsman authorities have various roles to perform with diverse forms of legitimacy.

5. Financial arrangements lack any form of integration and generally are specific to each agency and organisation. There is a distinct absence of any form of common or joint budgeting mechanisms to underpin collaborative projects and policies.

6. Data collection, storage and use are the subject of different systems, protocols and rationales – IT systems are often incompatible; rules affecting confidentiality prevent common use; data is collected in different spatial units and at different times – all making collaborative efforts difficult for middle managers and others.

The research studies referred to overleaf were all based on a case study approach (Yin, 1989). The bulk of the fieldwork involved in-depth interviews with middle managers, augmented by relevant documentary material in the form of policy documents, strategies and briefings. The sampling strategies were purposeful and opportunistic, capturing the experiences and views of middle managers from different departments, policy areas and professions, and with experiences of a diverse set of tri-sector collaborative associations at different levels of governance. The sample included middle managers with varying proportions of their time devoted to intra- and inter-organisational management, and the organisations represented included local councils, Local Health Boards, third sector agencies, the Police and the Fire and Rescue Service. The total number of middle managers included in this pool of interviews amounted to around 60.

The evidence from my research studies, supplemented by other evidence, suggests that there are broadly three themes that are integral, interrelated and highly influential in the work of middle managers engaged in collaborative work. These are the subject of Chapters 3, 4 and 5.

Figure 1.1: Collaborative management for middle managers

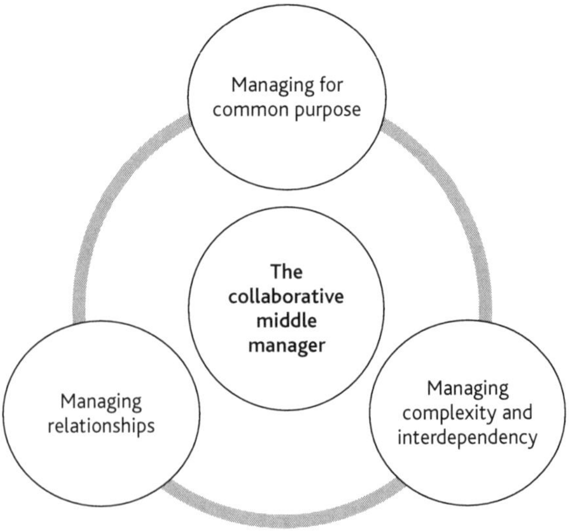

Chapter 3 concerns managing for common purpose. In sharp contrast to managing within agencies that is generally directed by clear purposes and aims, a major challenge for collaborative endeavours involves articulating, negotiating and securing common purpose between disparate actors and organisations.

The processes involved in developing a framework for future collaboration and direction – aims, goals, objectives, missions – demand purposeful and sensitive management behaviour and understanding. Critically, these need to be linked with notions of what constitutes success and positive outcomes for the different actors. An ability to understand why different actors want/need to engage in collaboration, and how different self-interests might be merged is key. Middle managers need an acute appreciation of the range of collaborators' interests and objectives, and an ability to manage these effectively through the various stages of the policy process. Mechanisms for linking strategic purpose with both service delivery and implementation, and meaningful outcome frameworks are an important part of the middle manager's collaborative repertoire. This chapter explores how common purpose is visualised, articulated, secured and evaluated through the role of middle managers, together with the framing processes implicit in these management behaviours.

Chapter 4 is devoted to managing complexity and interdependency. Undoubtedly, collaborative contexts present a highly challenging management framework that stems from the range and diversity of actors, sectors and organisations involved. Multi-organisational and cross-sector collaborations are constructed against a scaffolding of connections, interdependencies and networks. Understanding and appreciating this complex setting requires structural, technical and processual knowledge and competence in order to manage effectively. The components of this environment relate to financial and resource frameworks, organisational cultures, management systems, performance management regimes, institutional frameworks and the prevailing social, economic, political and environmental context. More fundamentally, middle managers need to appreciate the interlocking forces of structure, agency and ideas that frame their operating environment. Middle managers need to identify and assess the nature of interdependencies between actors and organisations, and they need to anticipate and manipulate connections to secure common purposes. Entrepreneurial, creative and innovative management behaviours are demanded throughout the policy cycle – strategy, delivery and evaluation – to manage these complex and interdependent settings.

Completing the main elements of managing for collaboration, Chapter 5 explores the practices and challenges of managing relationships with actors from diverse backgrounds, cultures, organisations, sectors, professions and life experiences. How do middle managers cultivate and sustain effective personal and professional relationships in a collaborative governance framework? What skills and competencies do they employ, and to what effect? Fundamental to these relationship processes are notions of power and trust which are manifested, contested, distributed and negotiated in different ways in collaborative contexts. Managing relationships is an important element of collaborative management with middle managers adopting bridging, gatekeeping, intermediary and filtering roles. Working in cross-boundary groups and building coalitions is an integral part of this form of management, but how exactly is this undertaken, what tactics and practices are the most effective, and why? This chapter also exposes the complex and ever-present dilemmas and ambiguities faced by middle managers particularly relating to multiple accountabilities, blurred personal and professional relationships, and differential notions of what constitutes success. Finally, the chapter reflects on the relationship between structure and agency and explores how relationship management might be hindered or enabled by different organisational and institutional frameworks.

Chapter 6 is broadly a comparative analysis determining the extent to which, if any, managing within organisations is similar to, or different from, managing between organisations. Unsurprisingly, there is no consensus on this important question, but rather a range of different positions along a continuum from generally the same to materially different. To some, this might seem somewhat academic, but if managing in collaboration is considered to be different in any way, it does have profound implications for policy, practice, training and development in public policy and management. At the very least, if managing in these contexts is different, this needs to be reflected in the future development of public middle managers.

Chapter 7 considers the implications of the preceding analysis and discussion for policy, practice and learning primarily for policy makers and managers/practitioners, but also for students, researchers and academics. The policy and practice community has a keen appetite for 'evidence-based policymaking' and 'what works' products and tools. Diverse forms of collaboration are regularly being designed as responses to emerging issues, funding opportunities, government initiatives and other stimuli; and existing collaborations are the subject of reflection and evaluation. Research insights that can be converted into good practice and policy advice should be welcome in this environment, including advice on what form of middle management in collaboration is the most effective, how it can be supported, what strategies work and conversely which are less effective. The implications of this research are considered in relation to the training, development and learning/knowledge management strategies of middle managers. This section also considers professional programmes, continuous development packages, skills/competency frameworks, secondment/mentoring opportunities, communities of practice and other potential initiatives designed to improve the capabilities of middle managers operating in this important arena of management. Finally, Chapter 8 brings the book to a conclusion with a summary and reflection of the main themes, arguments and perspectives examined in this book. It compiles a list of key lessons for middle managers working in collaborative environments, and reflects on their distinctiveness in comparison with other types of public manager. The book's contribution is considered in the context of the existing literature, and a future research agenda on this topic of study is set out in terms of research questions and themes, research methodologies and areas of study.

Key audience

There is a danger with a book of this nature of attempting to satisfy a range of audiences. There is a tension between the learning needs of academic and policy/practice communities – certainty and bias for action is important for policy makers/ practitioners leading to an appetite for prescriptions and simplifications, as opposed to academics who are more comfortable around ambiguity, analysis and theorising (Menzies, 2017). However, I believe that it is generally unhelpful to perpetuate the separation of the needs of these two communities, when a greater integration and dialogue between them would be beneficial to both. I understand that the focus of either may be different but their respective agendas are better addressed and practised in the light of each other's needs. With this in mind, the book has been written primarily for a policy and practitioner audience, but in a manner that offers a robust academic underpinning. It shies away from over-simplification but offers learning frameworks to stimulate individual and organisational learning. At the end of each chapter, is a summary of the key learning points and lessons for policy makers and practitioners, as well suggestions for future reading. In addition, an appendix offers a list of questions for discussion and debate primarily for use in group discussions and workshops. It is intended as a resource for both academics and trainers.

2

Public management and public managers

A new policy environment and new organisational arrangements should make co-operation and collaboration easier than it has been in the past. But real success will depend as much on the determination and creativity of practitioners and managers as it will on Government edict and structural change. (Poxton, 1993: 3)

This chapter opens with short overview of public management, focusing on its context and character, capturing the role of public managers in general operating in this environment, and specifically highlighting any references to the behaviours of middle managers. It proceeds to review the diverse and interdisciplinary contributions that form the theoretical backcloth to collaboration, before proceeding to examine the literature on management between organisations and the role of individual actors in this setting.

Public management

The purpose of this opening section is not to indulge in a lengthy discussion around the contested notion and nature of public management that can be readily found in numerous textbooks (Lynn, 2006; Osborne, 2010a), but simply to outline some relevant background to support and frame some of the later discussions addressed in this book. Historically, the design and delivery of public policy and management have been characterised by a number of dominant approaches – from Public Administration to New Public Management and, arguably, to New Public Governance – although in practice differences between these can be confused (Table 2.1).

The focus of public administration is on the delivery of public services prescribed by legislation, with public administrators governed by various rules and procedures. Here, there is a clear divide between politics and the administration; bureaucracy is central to making and delivering policy; and the role of professionals is dominant, reflecting the 'institutionalisation of the impartial expertise necessary to meet the complex, technical needs of the modern state' (Lynn, 2006: 260). In contrast, public management is driven more by public purposes and the process

Table 2.1: Main features of approaches to public management

	Main features	Management skills
Public administration	• Rules and procedures • Legal authority and duties • Hierarchy and bureaucracy • Central role of professionals and expertise • Application of traditional public service values • Clear separation between politics and administration	• Domain expertise • Command and control • Professionalism • Domain expertise
New Public Management	• Introduction of business and entrepreneurial disciplines from the private sector • Emphasis on efficiency, value for money, quality, measurable performance • Customer focus • Decentralisation	• Strategic management • Private sector skills relating to financial planning, performance management and human resource management
Public governance	• Appreciation of interdependencies between issues, organisations and citizens • Hollowing-out of government • Growth of networks and collaboration	• Network and collaborative management skills • Teamwork • Stakeholder engagement • Focus on personal relationships • Management of common purposes and complexity

of strategic choice (Ranson and Stewart, 1994: 34), and where management tasks involve policy planning, staff development, organisational development, engaging with the public, and reviewing and evaluating practices. Management is seen as a craft and the product of actions and decisions of public managers. Bovaid and Loffler (2003: 5) define public management as: 'an approach which uses managerial techniques to increase the value for money achieved by public services'. In contrast, the notion of New Public Management that gained traction from the 1970s, assumes that 'more businesslike and entrepreneurial management styles would lead to more efficient use of resources, citizens-as-consumers would be empowered and economies would be liberated' (Noordegraaf, 2015: 33). Learning from the private sector, entrepreneurial leadership and performance is important in this discourse. Osborne (2010b: 4) contends that this approach has led to 'the evolution of management as a coherent and legitimised role and function within Public Service Organisations, in contrast to (and often in conflict with) the traditional professional groupings'. Stacey (2010: 207) considers that power relations in organisations: 'are now tilted firmly towards the top of the hierarchy of managers and away from the professionals who actually deliver the service'. He goes on to argue that:

> The collegial form of public sector governance has all but vanished, or perhaps more accurately, is still practiced to some extent in the shadow of the legitimate surveillance. However, the particular form of power configuration which has emerged is sustained by a very different ideology to that which prevailed before. This is an ideology of efficiency, measurable quality and improvement, managerial control to produce uniformity of service; in short, an ideology of the market which takes precedence over the ideology of vocation.

The major criticism of New Public Management approaches centre on its intraorganisational focus and failure to appreciate the interdependent context of the prevailing public policy landscape. New Public Governance approaches are intended to correct this deficiency with mechanisms that involve citizens and other stakeholders to a much greater degree in decision-making processes. The focus here is on 'interorganisational relationships and upon the governance of processes, stressing service effectiveness and outcomes that rely upon the interaction of PSOs with their environment' (Osborne, 2010: 9b). In this context, accountability structures require negotiation and sources of power are dispersed and contested. Radin (2003) observes that the twenty-first century landscape for public management is very different from that in preceding years. This is because there has been a movement away from single policy issues to a focus on cross-cutting issues; a difference in views about the role of government and a 'hollowing-out' of government with contracting out of services, privatisation and a criticism of traditional bureaucratic structures; greater interdependence between levels of government; increased involvement from the private sector; and a focus on performance, accountability and scrutiny. This changed operating environment suggests the need for new management skills – away from managers defaulting into the traditional command and control models, more towards working in networks with other variably interdependent and committed actors and interests. Ranson and Stewart (1994: 150) argue that here, 'management of mutual influence is of more importance than the management of direct action' and certainly, managing outwards is a key competence for effective managers at all levels. However, a note of caution is expressed by Radin (2003: 347) who is somewhat sceptical about whether this has been adopted in practice because: 'intergovernmental dialogue continues to be characterised by a focus on separate programs, policies or organisations and a search for clarity and simplicity in the delineation of roles and responsibilities'. 6 et al (2006: 121) go further and argue that there is little difference, if any, between managing within and between organisations because:

> The goals of management are to arrange and coordinate resources, interests, commitments and sense-making to pursue the aspirations of a particular agency. This is undertaken within prevailing

constraints, such as, for example, the legal and contractual limits on the manner by which aims can be pursued. Management is an activity of trying to shape organisational ability, individual willingness and available resources in order to sustain collective action in pursuit of the objectives of either a single organisation or system or organisations.

The argument advanced here is that the basic tools of management are the same irrespective of context and structure. The authors also dispute the point that a manager's inability to exercise authority over others in an inter-organisational context is a crucial difference, because, even within organisations, there are only a limited number of occasions that a manager resorts to exercising control and authority over others, and it is often a strategy that is counter-productive in terms of staff motivation and trust. However, as we will see in Chapter 6, the debate around the contrasts and comparisons between intra- and inter-organisational management is keenly contested.

Public managers

Following the work of Moore (1995), O'Toole et al (2005) consider that public managers work in three broad directions to achieve their objectives – upwards and downwards to manage the internal affairs of the organisation; and outwards to link with an interdependent environment. Managing upwards and downwards is typically framed as a principal–agent relationship, whereas managing outwards is likely to be premised on a more collaborative and trust-based approach. O'Toole and Meier (2010: 325) also point to: 'efforts to limit the negative impact of environmental perturbations on the administrative system'. This refers to the implications of collaborative behaviour on core functions and practices of an organisation together with the possibilities of mainstreaming strategies. Van der Wal (2017) refers to three ideal types of public manager – the traditional, rule-orientated bureaucrat operating within a hierarchical, formalised and bureaucratic organisation with authority based on expertise and knowledge; the 'businesslike', performance-focused manager responding to the demands of New Public Management and embracing values of efficiency, value for money, market mechanisms and outsourcing; and, more recently, the networking, relation-focused collaborator who works with others to tackle cross-boundary issues and problems. He proceeds to map these ideal types against new, evolving and longstanding roles identified in the work of Needham and Mangan (2013) and Needham et al (2013) on the profile of the twenty-first century public manager. A particularly interesting point is raised about the longstanding role of the expert and whether: 'domain expertise is more or less important than generic management skills' (van der Wal, 2017: 28). Having identified the roles of public managers, van der Wal proceeds to attach a set of skills, competencies and values to each – traditional ones such as domain expertise, political astuteness and bargaining, and new ones to discharge a more collaborative turn such as networking, stakeholder engagement and teamwork.

Fulop and Linstead (2004: 7) consider that management at its root concerns the management of relationships, and because of this relational quality 'managers have to deal with multiple realities, roles and identities, and multiple loyalties to individuals'. Whereas traditional approaches to management focus on controlling relationships, modern approaches attempt to equalise these relationships for mutual advantage. Mintzberg (1975) produced a highly influential study of senior managers which identified managers engaged in three groups of roles – interpersonal, including performing as a figurehead, leader and liaison person; informational, as a pivotal point for the receipt and dissemination of information; and decisional, which entails being engaged in running the business. Although the research involved private sector managers at or near the top of organisations, it does have resonance in the present context. Indeed, Fulop and Linstead (2004: 10) apply this analysis specifically to middle managers and identify four key roles undertaken – creators and implementers of strategy; influencers by virtue of their confluence between vertical and horizontal communication; key sources of stability, perhaps even resistance to change, but certainly as a consolidator of change; and drivers of continual change. They further argue that managers exercise a set of performance skills by 'building and changing relationships based on managing power, meaning and knowledge' (Fulop and Linstead, 2004: 12) within a highly volatile societal and governance context, and need to 'surf' the waves of changing relationships to avoid 'the vertigo' of possibilities to act effectively. Again, in a private sector context, Balogun (2003: 71) considers that middle managers are a strategic asset and, in addition to the implementation of deliberate strategies, they:

> use their position within the organisation and their contacts externally to gather and synthesize information for strategic managers on threats and opportunities; encourage fledgling projects within their own departments to help facilitate adaptability within the organisation; and use resources at their disposal to champion innovative ideas and business opportunities to senior managers.

Haneberg (2010: 6) maintains that a middle manager's role includes: 'a broad range of tasks such as planning, goal setting, performance management, problem solving, process improvement, relationship building, analysis, communication updates, budgeting, and decision making'. She further asserts that: 'middle management is a craft, a set of practices, and a job that managers learn with the right training and guidance. Good middle managers are cultivated, not born' (Haneberg, 2010: 11); and summing up the main characteristics of an effective middle manager, she lists being accountable and taking ownership; making a contribution to organisational goals; being a role model; focusing on results; working in partnership with others; working flexibly in teams; facilitating the work of others; and being responsive to the ideas and concerns of others.

Traditional views of middle managers often visualise them as: 'linking pins', or a conduit, connecting senior managers with the rest of the organisation and relaying senior manager orders in an unquestioning fashion, and needing to be proficient in management techniques associated with control such as budgeting and project management. However, middle managers are also still subject to much criticism as resistant, foot dragging, self-seeking, saboteurs of change' (Balogun, 2007: 82), who are protective of their own interests and reluctant implementers of change conceived by top management when they are considered not to be in their best interests. McGurk (2009: 465) considers that middle managers occupy a pivotal midway position in an organisation between frontline staff and top management enabling them to offer an important contribution to organisational continuity and change, requiring a fine balance of both management and leadership skills and knowledge. He argues that: 'on the one hand, MMs require the skills to control people and resources to implement business plans; on the other they also need the ability to reflect upon their experiences and relationships with others and work effectively with staff to deliver strategic changes, both those driven from the top and those initiated from below'. Clarke et al (2007: 94) reflect on the duality of a role experienced by middle managers as having 'a peculiar loneliness', where they are managing as well as being managed. They suggest that the notion of what it means to be a middle manager has become problematic, particularly in situations where non-managerial staff have been encouraged 'to become more "self-managing" and managers have been encouraged to become coaches rather than overseers, which has increased managers' accountability to staff' and 'and trends may have led managers to identify more with their colleagues at work than the organisations that employ them'. This point is underscored by Huy (2002: 61) who argues that middle managers, more so than senior executives, have an emotional balancing role to play, particularly in times of change because they are: 'structurally closer to their employees and so are likely to be more attuned to their subordinates' emotional needs'. Mayer and Smith (2007: 79) are under no illusions that: 'it is middle management in particular that ultimately defines the real and realized outcomes of change' and that organisations need to recognise this much more in their approaches to planning and change management. Similarly, within the context of strategic change, research by Balogun (2003) suggests that middle managers should be viewed as 'change intermediaries' who absorb and cope with change. This involves sense making with the interpretation and translation of the intentions of change being processed for themselves and for their staff and teams. It involves acting as role models, making sense of the implications of change on different boundaries and responsibilities, handling resistance and providing assistance in the form of coaching, training and support. These roles are particularly effective when discharged within informal processes of communication. Floyd and Wooldridge (1994: 48) observe that:

> typically, middle managers have been seen as part of an organization's control system. Middle management does things that translate strategies defined at higher levels into actions at operating levels. This involves: (1) defining tactics and developing budgets for achieving a strategy; (2) monitoring the performance of individuals and subunits; and (3) taking corrective action when behavior falls outside expectations.

However, this ignores another major role so that now 'middle managers perform a coordinating role where they mediate, negotiate and interpret connections between the organisation's institutional (strategic) and technical (organisational) levels' (Floyd and Wooldridge, 1997: 466). They act as 'linking pins' between vertically related groups and exert strategic influence in two directions – upwards through synthesising information by framing and interpretation, and championing new programmes and opportunities; and downwards, by facilitating adaptability and implementing strategy. These authors maintain that middle managers act as buffers between operating level initiatives and the scrutiny of top management; champion initiatives to top management when 'the time is right'; and finally, they suggest that their strategic influence is enhanced if they are located in boundary spanning units because of their ability to mediate between the internal and external environment. However, this capability can vary according to different contexts and circumstances, and middle managers in non-boundary spanning units can sometimes be equally influential.

Currie and Procter (2005: 1325) take the view that: 'organisational performance is heavily influenced by what happens in the middle of organisations, rather than at the top'.

Especially in the context of strategic action, they concur with the perspectives taken by Floyd and Wooldridge (1997) and agree that middle managers participate in both strategy design and implementation. More specifically, their involvement can be of four types – synthesising information, championing alternatives, facilitating adaptability and implementing deliberate strategy. The last type involves defining managerial actions consistent with strategic intent, converting strategy into action plans and individual objectives, and coordinating the various elements of change required. They also reinforce the point made by Floyd and Wooldridge (1997) that middle managers have a greater effect on organisational performance when they are involved in setting goals and generating alternatives than when they are involved purely in the implementation side of the process. Furthermore, where middle managers occupy boundary-spanning positions with connections to outside agencies and service recipients, they are likely to be particularly well positioned to offer informed analysis and contributions to strategy. There is an important proviso to this in the view of Currie and Procter in relation to professional bureaucracies in public services. They counsel that: 'the presence of a powerful professional group limits the potential for middle managers to move from a "diplomat" role to a more autonomous strategic role' (2005: 1351). As most public services organisations are still heavily influenced by professional elites and groups, this needs to be recognised.

Westley (1990: 339) also picks up the point about involvement and inclusion in organisational strategy and argues that:

> middle managers can impede the implementation process if they do not perceive it as being in their interests to cooperate, and they respond in organisationally dysfunctional ways to perceived powerlessness. On the other hand, when this group is permitted to exert influence the result may be a more responsive, innovative organisation.

She argues that middle managers are likely to feel more included and energised about strategic issues if they are involved in strategic decision-making processes, and not excluded because of status, control and hierarchical issues. Again, in a similar vein, Spreitzer and Quinn (1996) contend that the traditional roles of middle managers must change to become more strategic than operational; to concentrate more on generating and mobilising resources and new ideas, and engaging in strategy making. In particular, they argue that 'their role must shift from transactional managers charged with maintaining the status quo to transformational leaders who stimulate change' (Spreitzer and Quinn, 1996: 238), and as Uhl-Bien and Arena (2018: 91) assert: 'middle managers need to be conceived as "organisational connectors" who create linkages that enable transitions from one system to another'. However, the prospect of stimulating middle managers to become transformational agents of change are problematic – dependent upon individual characteristics of the manager such as self-esteem, and organisational characteristics such as barriers to change and the availability of social support. Spreitzer and Quinn (1996: 256) conclude that, 'if senior management is serious about unleashing the transformational energy of the "frozen middle", it must pay attention to the feelings of middle managers'.

Friedman (2001) provides an interesting perspective on managers in the context of their contribution to organisational learning. He explores the role of individuals as 'agents' of organisational learning or 'intrapreneurs'. Friedman argues that a profile of agents for organisational learning needs to reflect contradictory characteristics – proactive but reflective; having high aspirations but being realistic about the limitations of organisational complexity and the forces resisting change; critical but committed and loyal to the organisation; and independent but very cooperative with others. In some ways, the role of agent exceeds job descriptions and it 'may be risky and requires a particular set of attributes and skills for dealing with the conflict and resistance that learning often engenders' (Friedman, 2001: 412). However, the potential benefits are significant for both the organisation and the individual manager.

Acknowledging the importance of promoting inclusion within public management, Feldman and Khademian (2007) focus on the role of the public manager in practising inclusive management. This involves balancing three foundational perspectives – political, scientific/expert, and local or experienced-based – although these have to be tempered by additional organisational, sectoral and interest-based factors. Feldman and Khademian (2007: 309) argue that:

> the responsibility for combining these sometimes disparate perspectives in the efforts to address public problems implies a different role for public managers than the role implied by any of the three models taken separately. They are not simply in charge of execution as in the political oversight model, nor are they primarily advisors and decision makers as in the expertise model, and they are not principally facilitators as in the models of public participation. Instead, these managers 'assume the roles of steward, teacher, and designer whose functions are…to ensure a process in which generative learning can take place'. (Roberts, 1997: 125)

Fundamental to inclusive management is the informational and relational work that public managers need to undertake, performing roles of broker, translator and synthesiser, in order to understand problems, design effective solutions and work together with all the constituent stakeholders.

The context of collaboration

One of the main changes that has occurred in the governance, design and delivery of public services around the world over the last 50 years has been the steady growth of collaborative forms of working. This has resulted in different collaborative permutations between agencies from the public, private and third sectors, which have infiltrated most policy areas and tiers of governance in various degrees of intensity, character and form. As Ansell and Torfing (2015: 315) suggest:

> Although hierarchies and markets continue to play a crucial role in regulating society and the economy and

delivering public and private services, collaborative forms of governance are proliferating, fuelled by institutional complexity and political fragmentation and driven by the recognition that no single actor has the knowledge or resources to solve complex societal problems.

However, research into this area is sometimes hampered by the absence of definitional consensus on the term 'collaboration' and the use of many other expressions that are in frequent use to describe forms of inter-organisational working such as 'strategic alliance', 'partnership', 'network' and 'integration'. One straightforward definition of collaboration is: 'any joint activity that is intended to produce more public value than could be produced when the agencies act alone' (GAO, 2012a: 3) A popular approach to theorising about collaboration is to locate it along a continuum that seeks to capture the intensity of relationships between the actors involved – cooperation, coordination, collaboration and integration or merger – although there are other versions of this model. Sandfort and Milward (2008) also distinguish collaboration at different levels – policy, organisational, programme and client. The consequence of this form of organising has been described as: 'co-configuration' characterised by complex, multi-professional settings involving a distribution of expertise away from compact teams and professional networks to 'knotworking' – 'a rapidly changing, partially improvised collaboration of performance between otherwise loosely connected professionals' (Warmington et al, 2004: 4).

The attendant literature on theorising collaboration is diverse, hampered by considerable inter-disciplinary variety particularly from the fields of sociology, economics and political science. However, this may not be altogether problematic because the value of inter-disciplinary variety is that it can shine an inquiring light onto a very complex field and yield insights and perspectives that may be hidden by a single focus. Augmenting this mainstream disciplinary theorising of collaboration, are a plethora of models and frameworks that have been developed based on a number of different parameters including types of collaboration, motivation, structural form, stages or phases in the process of collaboration, and factors or themes influencing the shape and trajectory of collaboration – including barriers and enablers. The material on factors and themes are particularly popular for policy makers, managers and practitioners who have a keen appetite for 'what works' guidance in their complex challenge of managing in this form of governance. Countless 'good practice guides' have been compiled emphasising the importance of articulating and negotiating clear purpose and objectives; developing trust and sharing power; managing accountability and performance; sharing and distributing leadership; building boundary spanning competencies; and developing learning and knowledge management strategies.

A material feature of collaboration and collaborative governance concerns the issue of scale (Ansell and Torfing, 2015), the dimensions of which can be geographical, temporal, jurisdictional, functional or operational. Collaboration can operate at a single scale or multiple scales and move dynamically between them. The challenges of operating at these different scales can be theorised in terms of membership, interaction (frequency, type, duration) and strategic horizon (short or long term), and it is likely that they increase with scale because of transaction costs, the greater diversity and complexity inherent in the assembly of more stakeholders, and the problems of developing and sustaining trust-based relationships between them. Scale may be an important influence at different stages in the policy process with 'scaling-up' important at the policy design stage, and 'scaling-down' more relevant at the policy implementation phase. Collaboration is likely to present issues of 'scale' to middle managers who have only previously experienced working within the boundaries of their own organisations. Critically, collaboration most frequently occurs within systems of fragmented governance creating: 'situations in which an authority's incentives do not align with collectively desired outcomes, arise from spillovers of policy choice and design that transcend jurisdictions' (Swann and Kim, 2018: 274). Viewed through the lens of Institutional Collective Action, these lead to various dilemmas relating to inefficient behaviour and undesirable outcomes that are indeed:

ubiquitous in governance. They manifest *horizontally* between governmental units at the same level as the consequences of one unit's actions spill over to another's jurisdiction); *vertically* as a governmental unit at one level pursues complementary or conflicting actions to those pursued at a higher or lower level; and *functionally* between subunits of a unitary authority. (p. 274)

Various strategies have been deployed to address these dilemmas in relation to facilitating collaborative governance: 'including power symmetry, incentive alignment, participant commitment, face-to-face dialogue, shared understanding and motivation, well-defined rules, effective leadership, flexible policy solutions, legitimacy and capacity for joint action' (p. 274). In response, Swann and Kim (2018) list a number of practical suggestions to reduce collaboration risk, uncertainty, transaction costs and to promote more self-organised integration including, increasing face-to-face networking and fostering reciprocal relations; crafting collaborative strategies around service characteristics; exploiting commonalities with partners; increasing transparency, accountability and equality through inclusiveness; and developing collective capacity through incrementalism.

The clear message is that a collaborative context presents a very particular set of conditions and parameters that need to be addressed by a combination of both structural and agential components. Although the thrust of this book is on the agency of middle managers in collaboration, it is necessary to frame this within a wider context and their interplay with structural factors. The structure–agency debate is keenly contested and unfortunately often presented as a dichotomy. From a more pragmatic position, Williams and Sullivan (2009) advance the view that while actors manufacture outcomes, the parameters of their capacity to act – the constraints and opportunities – is set by the structural context within which they operate. The components of structure include the social, economic and environmental drivers; statutory, institutional and financial context; accountability, governance and performance management structures; organisational and professional cultures;

and collaboration capital – the accumulation of social and network capital built up over time. These present a complicated and dynamic set of forces that interact with agency – they frame, inhibit, enable, constrain, influence, inspire, sway and provide the scaffolding for managerial approaches, behaviours and actions. The key task for politicians and policy makers intent on securing successful collaborative working is to provide a supportive structural context to enable effective agential orientations through a combination of positive enabling factors and by the removal of any barriers. Arguably, especially in a UK context, successive governments have tended to intervene with countless structural changes – organisational re-configurations and re-organisations, statutory duties and various financial initiatives – without necessarily being clear on their effects on agency. This is in part understandable because of the difficulties of attributing causality between the constituent factors. Although the outcomes of collaboration are heavily influenced through the complicated interplay of structure and agency, it should also be acknowledged that ideational influences play a role. Certain narratives, stories, policy paradigms and ideas – often dominating at specific times – can influence approaches to the design and delivery of public services. 'Joined-up government' and 'citizen-centred services' are two such recent examples that have had a profound impact on public policy and management.

The organisation and management of public services, especially in the UK, has undergone various transformations over recent decades. From a situation that was largely dominated by hierarchical and bureaucratic forms, the organisational landscape was first exposed to the discipline of the private sector with the introduction of market-based solutions, and then to the imperatives and attractions of working in networks resulting in the various manifestations of collaboration. Now, the organisational and governance landscape is a complicated mosaic of these three types of organising, co-existing in different policy areas, areas of administration and stages of the policy process. The demands of management and managers in these different organisational types varies significantly, although there can be similarities. A central theme of this book is that managing in collaborative settings presents a series of challenges not faced in the other forms of organising – although as a Chapter 6 explores, the extent of this divergence is somewhat contested. Nevertheless, it is important to devote some time to set out the essential nature and characteristics of this form of organising, and to touch on some of the main theories that attempt to explain this phenomenon.

Without indulging too deeply in matters of terminology, and as has been mentioned previously, it is important to note at the outset, that there are many understandings of the notion of 'collaboration' and that numerous other terms are used liberally to refer to forms of inter-organisational working. Suffice it to say, that particularly for policy makers and managers, it is very important to be clear on what is meant by whatever terms are used and to communicate these clearly with others. The essential point to emphasise is that a collaborative context and setting consists of a number of ingredients that are likely to be highly influential and instrumental in shaping the subsequent management approaches and behaviours. These stem from the fact that collaboration involves actors and stakeholders gathered together from a range of different types of background and agency, resulting in differences in attitude and experiences towards key aspects of the collaborative process including:

- **Motivation** – a potent elixir of effectiveness, efficiency and responsiveness discourses (Sullivan et al, 2012a), underpin the main motivations of actors working in collaboration. Additional complexity is supplied by the dynamic and changing nature of these discourses as a result of prevailing views and government policy. This policy can take the form of exhortation or more forcefully by mandate through statutory duties, financial incentives and other prescriptions. An interesting point centres on the value of mandated collaboration and whether compelling actors and interests to work together actually is the best strategy? This can result in token forms of collaboration and other forms of resistance if actors consider it not to be in their best interests. An equally important reflection relates to an appreciation that collaboration involves both benefits and costs, and that a blinkered crusade promoting the unchallenged virtues of collaboration is not warranted in all forms of public service design and delivery. A collaborative approach requires careful appraisal because there is considerable evidence to suggest that the process can be tortuous, protracted, resource-intensive and often resulting in a failure to deliver on expectations (Cook, 2015).

- **Purpose and objectives** – given the mixture of motivations and drivers underpinning collaborative endeavours, it is little wonder that the purposes and objectives of the different stakeholders involved can vary and fluctuate. 6 et al (2006) suggest that apart from being framed structurally, goals may be framed instrumentally, in terms of resources to be accessed or outputs desired, relationally, in terms of the relationships sought with other parties, and narratively, in terms of the impact on sense-making around the notion of collaboration. Goal incongruence is a familiar feature of many collaborations and an enduring challenge is to negotiate clear and unambiguous common purposes that can provide a coherent way forward for the individual actions of partners. A common criticism of many collaborative strategies is that their missions are too nebulous and their objectives too numerous, not prioritised or capable of measurement. The tricky problem is being able to balance the need to demonstrate clarity of purpose sufficient for all parties to sign up to, with sufficient flexibility to prevent paralysis through incompatible disputes. Goals also have a tendency to shift as a result of new challenges, ongoing performance issues or changes in government direction. The outcomes of collaboration and 'what constitutes success' may be different for different stakeholders. Service users will naturally judge success in terms of the quality of the service they receive; whereas funders may be more interested in the most cost-effective use of resources; and strategists will look to achieving policy coherence and lack of duplication.
- **Power** – a key feature of collaborative environments is the diffuse, contested and distributed nature of power relationships. Although the operating rules of collaboratives suggest equal standing of each member, in practice, there are power differentials between them that represent

significant challenges. Bryson and Crosby (1992: 323) refer to a situation of 'no-one-in-charge', because the typical single and sovereign sources of power that can be found within single organisations – particularly as a product of the sedimentation of power within hierarchical structures – cannot be entertained in collaboration. 6 et al (2006) point to four basic instruments of power – control, inducement, suasion and coping – and while the exercise of these can be strongly associated with different types of organisational and institutional context – for example, control with hierarchies and suasion with collective action – all are possible options for managers and leaders. The consequence of this for leadership and managerial behaviours and actions is profound in terms of the strategies they adopt in any particular situation and at any one time.

• **Culture, values and operating systems** – diversity and variety between partners in collaboration stem from fundamental attitudes and practices relating to value systems, professional and organisational cultures, and the resultant operating systems of management and organisation. Tri-sectoral collaboration present the greatest challenges with different understandings of public value and the rights and responsibilities of citizens and communities. These are embedded and ingrained in subsequent organisational cultures that are notoriously difficult to shift and change over time, despite persistent organisational re-designs and structural re-configurations. The clash of professional cultures is a further source of contestation such as those exhibited within settings of integrated health and social care. These stem from fundamental differences even to the notion of 'health' itself and spawn sub-cultures between different health and social care professionals, practitioners and managers. Attitudes and perceptions of the recipients of service or the 'public' are also a potential source of conflict between different interests.

• **Legal and financial frameworks/roles and responsibilities** – theatres of collaboration bring together agencies that are the subject of defined statutory roles and responsibilities underpinned and framed within a tight envelope of legal and financial parameters. These can be at odds with the ambitions of collaboration because they must be the first call on an individual organisation's legitimacy and probity.

• **Accountability and performance** – collaborative settings are characterised by a condition of contorted oversight with different systems of performance and scrutiny. Accountabilities are likely to be multiple and sometimes conflicting because of the range of different types of organisation involved – some public, some third sector and sometimes private. Even within a family of public sector agencies working together, the situation is often unclear and problematic as a result of different performance management systems and forms of scrutiny. It becomes even more complicated when partnering agencies hail from different levels of governance and are responsible for administrative areas that are not coterminous. Agencies are 'held to account' in different ways depending on their sectoral affiliation. Public sector agencies are rooted in systems of democratic accountability through formally elected bodies – each with their own systems of decision-making and scrutiny – some of which can be perceived as cumbersome and overly bureaucratic. Third sector organisations embrace a variety of models that are set up to represent their particular interests, and private sector organisations are clearly accountable to their shareholders. This mix of accountabilities is often the source of tension and confusion particularly where they conflict with one another, where they influence the speed of decision making, and where they create confusion and perceptions of lack of transparency by the recipients of collaborative action and policy. Attributing responsibility in multi-party collaborations can be a source of puzzlement for service recipients, but also a cause of friction between partners.

So, the context of collaboration presents public managers with an operating environment that is significantly different to the ones they face within the boundaries of their own organisations. It is certainly more complex and the differences inherent in the partners they are likely to encounter across a number of parameters present huge challenges in the pursuit of common purposes. The significance of this different operating environment is that managers face challenges as a consequence of working both within and between organisations. Connelly et al (2008), O'Leary and Bingham (2007) and O'Leary (2015) list these as:

- balancing autonomy and interdependence – sometimes working independently by setting rules and making decisions, but recognising that membership of a collaborative network requires an acceptance that they are entwined in a collective decision-making structure;
- recognising that collaborative managers and their networks have both common and diverse goals – unique to an individual member's organisation or programme and common to a network's shared goals;
- working both with a fewer number and a greater variety of groups that are increasingly more diverse – when organisations combine to form a network, they become one body – hence the fewer number. Yet within this one body typically is a great variety of organisations with different cultures, missions and ways of operating – hence the greater diversity;
- needing to be both authoritative and participative – sometimes leading and commanding, but at others being more facilitative and participative;
- balancing advocacy with inquiry – sometimes promoting and advocating on behalf of their own organisation, but at other times, sponsoring the best interest of the collaboration;
- attending to detail as well as the whole picture – appreciating the need for a clear vision and whole-systems thinking, but also attending to the details of making it happen, particularly in their own organisation.

Management in collaboration

Hibbert et al (2008) outline the different research approaches, methodologies and underlying theories that have been used to study management in collaboration. They identify three ways in which collaboration is conceptualised – life-cycles, phases and stages; typologies, models and diagnostics; and success and failure factors – before proceeding to categorise the management responses – competencies, behaviours and tasks; guidelines and process steps; tools and facilitation; and themes and reflective practice. A fundamental difference is made by numerous researchers (Agranoff and McGuire, 2001; O'Toole, 1996; Goldsmith and Eggers, 2004) between managing in hierarchies to managing in collaboration, suggesting that traditional approaches to public administration are no longer relevant to working in this context. A stream of research and practice has been gathered around the notion of 'collaborative public management' that is defined as

> a concept that describes the process of facilitating and operating in multiorganisational arrangements to solve problems that cannot be solved or easily solved by single organisations. Collaborative means to *co-labor*, to cooperate to achieve common goals, working across boundaries in multisector relationships. Cooperation is based on the value of reciprocity. (O'Leary et al, 2006: 7)

Also, network management approaches have been promoted to capture the particular demands and challenges of managing in this form of organising. The literature on network management is, however, diverse, but Herranz (2008) has helpfully summarised the different approaches into four broad perspectives representing a passive-to-active continuum of managerial behaviour encompassing reactive facilitation, contingent coordination, active coordination and hierarchical-based directive administration. The reactive facilitation perspective is best represented by Kickert et al (1997) in which 'they adopt the archetypal view of networks as mostly loosely coupled weak-tied multiorganisational sets and suggest a passive, reactive, facilitative role for the public network manager' (Herranz, 2008: 4). Klijn (2005), influenced by the earlier work of Hanf and Scharpf (1978) considers the distinctive features of working in networks as follows:

- The power structure is divided between different actors, and individual actors have only limited authority over others. This implies a mutual dependency between actors that requires cooperative behaviours.

- The prevailing goal structure lacks clarity and uniformity because different organisations pursue different goals, so raising the importance of seeking rather than setting goals. The outcome can resemble a 'package deal, where different actors, find interesting elements that suit their interests and capabilities, rather than a unified common goal' (Klijn, 2005: 268).

- The role of the manager becomes one of mediator, and facilitator rather than system controller.

- Management activities coalesce around goal finding and accommodation; making organisational arrangement; and coordinating.

Klijn (2008: 132, emphasis in original) argues that, 'in sum, *the role of the manager* from an inter-organisational network perspective is equivalent to that of a mediator, a process manager, or a facilitator'.

The second perspective identified by Herranz (2008) is referred to as 'contingent coordination' reflecting a mixing of passive and actively limited managerial roles. Here, 'managers may exert some coordinating influence on networks, but the scope of managerial behavior is limited and contingent upon network interests, resources, and opportunities' (Herranz, 2008: 5). McGuire (2002) summarises the behaviours managers adopt in this perspective of network management as activation, involving identifying the actors and resources needed to achieve network goals; framing, focusing on the 'behaviours used to arrange and integrate a network structure by facilitating agreement on participants' roles, operating rules, and network values' (p. 603); and finally, synthesising which majors on building relationships and interactions.

The third perspective of network management is termed 'active coordination' where networks may be directly managed through four broad behaviours – activation, framing, mobilising and synthesising. Here, 'managers possess discretion in employing a variety of techniques to actively coordinate networks' but 'like its more passive cousins, active coordination does not have the same organisational controls traditionally associated with single-agency hierarchical public administration' (Herranz, 2008: 7). The final perspective is 'hierarchical-based directive administration' which is based on the presumption that there are some unique considerations to take into account in managing networks but these are not sufficient to demand different managerial actions. Herranz (2008: 8) points out that:

> all along the network management continuum, public managers face challenges to multiorganisational coordination such as goal incongruence, imprecise oversight, miscommunication, fragmented coordination, data deficits, capacity shortages, and relationship instability. Consequently, network managers encounter a range of strategic and managerial role choices depending on network structure, composition, and policy outcome expectations. In this situation, network management strategies are likely to be more effective if they more fully account for network composition and conditions.

Milward and Provan (2006:11) take the view that: 'public managers must understand what type of network they are managing and what its purpose is before they can manage it effectively', and they refer to four types of public networks – service implementation networks, information diffusion networks, problem solving networks, and community capacity building networks. They also differentiate between two types of network manager – one that is dedicated to the network as a whole, its organisation, servicing and coordination; and the other, more frequent in number: 'who represent their organisation within the network. They are managers whose primary loyalty is to their organisation, but who must work within a network context, addressing both organisation- and network-level goals and objectives. These managers have split missions and, sometimes, split loyalties'. This latter group is likely to include the vast majority of middle managers that represent the focus of this book. Milward and Proven (2006) set out a number of key management tasks for both types of manager that are interpreted in different ways. In relation to the managers *in* networks these involve

- the management of accountability: ensuring that the organisation has the appropriate buy-in to the network in terms of resources, facilities and staff; but also, ensuring that benefits are fairly levered into the organisation;
- the management of legitimacy: accepting that there is a responsibility to build and maintain the legitimacy of a network and to market and profile it within an organisation;
- the management of conflict: acting as 'linking pins' with other network managers to ensure problems and conflicts are resolved;
- the management of design: to be flexible within different network design and be adaptable to change, and in particular to act appropriately within different forms of network governance whether of the self-governing type or more centralised type such as a lead organisation;
- the management of commitment: to reflect the need to institutionalise network relations and not overly rely on personal ties; to mainstream relations into organisational decision-making processes, build support and disseminate information at different levels.

The implications of a network structure are that management strategies are diverse, focusing respectively on the management of interactions and the management of the network itself (Kickert et al, 1997; Agranoff and McGuire, 2001). O'Toole (1996), using rational choice theory, offers some interesting strategies for managers operating in networks including facilitating/altering the strategic game; influencing preferences through persuasion and building trust through reciprocity and mutual respect; and shifting the structure of the collaboration itself. Radin (2007) refers to the notion of 'intergovernmental management' to capture the managerial responses required to operate effectively in a policy environment characterised by an increase in boundary-spanning activities, shifting policy boundaries, shifting views about the role of government, interdependence between levels of government, public–private interdependence, and a focus on performance. She argues that this calls for new management skills particularly around bargaining to facilitate relationships that reject the traditional command and control paradigm embedded in hierarchies; and networking that seeks to involve a range of actors or 'a web of largely autonomous participants with variable degrees of mutual commitment or dependence on each other' (Radin, 2007: 367). This is the issue network approach (first promoted by Heclo, 1979) that:

> provides a way to include various interests in a process, cutting both horizontally (across multiple issues) as well as vertically (down the intergovernmental chain). It also establishes a framework that is responsive to the transient nature of policy coalitions, with various networks established for a particular situation but dissolved when that situation changes. (Radin, 2007: 367)

The collaborative manager

Sullivan and Skelcher (2002: 100) discuss the skills and attributes possessed by dedicated public managers who operate in collaborative settings – the so-called boundary spanners or reticulists who 'establish, facilitate and co-ordinate collaboration' through a critical appreciation of environment and problems/opportunities presented; an understanding different organisational contexts; knowing the role and playing it; communication; prescience; networking; negotiating; conflict resolution; risk-taking; problem-solving; and self-management. They also highlight the importance of such individuals in developing trust, and adopting a particular approach to leadership. Williams (2012a) refers to the importance of boundary spanners and boundary spanning behaviours in collaborative arenas where activities, processes and tasks permeate, bridge and cut across conventional boundaries of organisation, profession, sector and policy. Noble and Jones (2006) observe similar actors in the context of public–

private partnerships. Williams (2012a) argues that boundary spanners discharge a number of key roles – reticulist, interpreter/communicator, coordinator and entrepreneur – with a high degree of interplay and connectivity between them, and each demanding a particular set of skills and competencies:

- the reticulist role that focuses on the management of relationships and interdependencies highlighting the skills of diplomacy, negotiation, network management and influencing without formal power, sometimes referred to as 'informational intermediaries' or 'gatekeepers';
- the interpreter/communicator function that centres on an appreciation of the diversity of actors and their backgrounds, and an ability to liaise and connect with different and changing interests. At the heart of this role is the ability to build and sustain effective interpersonal relationships using the skills of communication, listening, empathy, conflict management and consensus seeking. Cultivating trusting behaviours is paramount in these processes;
- the coordinator role that majors on the planning, servicing and coordination of the collaborative process;
- the entrepreneurial function that focuses on the importance of developing new solutions to complex problems evidencing creativity, opportunism and innovation. This role is not just a technical one relating to ideas and resources, but also a personal and political one involving building coalitions and brokering deals among disparate interests.

Carey et al (2019) look to develop a typology of boundary spanners based on motivation and ways of operating. Four different types are advanced and referred to as: 'traditional', 'looking for an edge', 'moving on up' and 'pushing the ideas'. From their research in New Zealand, Ryan et al (2008) consider that a trio of roles (not necessarily a single individual) – the public entrepreneur, their guardian angel(s), and their fellow travellers – are necessary to form the core of collaborative management – working in an innovative, learning-orientated and networked fashion.

Donahue and Zeckhauser (2008) argue that orchestrating collaborative arrangements demands particular skills, the foremost of which are analytical and these 'have relatively little to do with classic public administration and a great deal to do with economics, institutional analysis, game theory, decision analysis, and other relatively advanced tools for predicting and influencing outcomes' (Donahue and Zeckhauser 2008: 522). In more detail, Donahue (2004) suggests that a collaborative governance pedagogy might usefully centre around six categories of professional skills listed in Box 2.1.

Box 2.1: Professional skills for collaborative governance

Appraisal: calibrating the dimensions of a governance challenge and the defects of the status quo in the absence of collaborative efforts to address it

Analysis: appreciating, in a sophisticated way, the forces at work in the policy area; identifying the incentives and predicting the behaviour of the actors within it

Assignment: selecting the institutional players to be recruited into or tasked with a particular responsibility within a collaborative system (to the extent the organisational constellation is malleable)

Architecture: designing a structure of information flows, financial relationships, and accountability arrangements with the best odds of focusing the collaboration's energies on real sources of public value

Assessment: evaluating the collaboration, to whatever level of precision permitted by the available data and the degree of normative clarity and consensus that exists

Adjustment: deploying formal or informal authority, guided by analysis and assessment, to fine-tune the structure, targeting, or operations of the collaboration

Source: Donahue, 2004

From the evidence of O'Leary and Gerard's (2012) research on US Federal senior executives, the skill set of the successful collaborator is considered to consist of *individual attributes* including, having an open mind, patience and self-confidence; *interpersonal* skills of being a good communicator, an excellent listener and working well with people; *group process skills* including, facilitation, negotiation and collaborative problem-solving; *strategic leadership skills* including, big-picture thinking, strategic thinking and facilitative leadership; and finally, *substantive/technical expertise* including technical knowledge of the subject area, project management and organisational skills. In a further clarification of this skill set, O'Leary et al (2012) argue that their research reinforces previous literature in this field but with one major caveat – that is, the importance of individual attributes such as flexibility, unselfishness, persistence, diplomacy, trustworthiness, honesty, friendliness and others. They use the term 'attribute' to denote an individual characteristic that is not necessarily fixed, rather than 'trait' that is inborn and resistant to change. They argue

> that people, process, and communication skills are not enough. In addition, successful collaboration requires an individual with an intricate set of relational attributes. Our analysis suggests that our SES respondents are sophisticated situational leaders and managers who have learned which attributes to use in particular situations in order for a collaboration to succeed. (O'Leary et al, 2012: S81)

Bingham and O'Leary (2006: 163) summarise McGuire's (2006) view of the unique skills of collaborative public management as activation, or identifying the right people and resources; framing, to get agreement on leadership, administrative roles and network identity; mobilising players, to get commitment and build relationships; and synthesising, to structure the network and link people. Other competencies include coaching, negotiation, mediation, building trust, interpersonal communications, and team building. He reports that public managers use many of the same skills as they do in managing single organisations, such as having the right people in the right places, communicating, inclusive strategic planning, organising and disseminating information and resolving conflict. An ARACY Factsheet (2013a: 3) maintains that:

> in essence, collaborative management involves building coalitions, mobilizing support and developing new ways to cope with strategic and operational complexity. Traditional management techniques are replaced by an emphasis on shaping and influencing relationships and driving these toward collaborative advantage and achieving the collaboration's goals. Most importantly, collaborative management is focused on leveraging strong relationships to create better outcomes.

Agranoff (2012) offers a wealth of operational advice/tips to network practitioners based on his engagement with actors over a long career – this ranges widely to include being patient; confronting power; building trust; developing multiple communication vehicles; being a decision broker to build consensus; looking to achieve small wins; sharing the network administrative burden; being creative, to name but a few. He takes the view that: 'the network effort will only be as good as the skills, experience, and knowledge of the persons sent by an organisation to be at the table' and reinforces his view that: 'public service in formal networks requires considerable knowledge and commitment to a process that is different from that of hierarchical management. Yet it is nevertheless management, across the boundaries of organisations' (2012: 58). In a guide for managers working in collaborative networks, Milward and Provan (2006) highlight the central tasks as managing accountability, legitimacy, conflict, design and commitment. Agranoff (2006) has compiled a list of ten lessons for public managers contemplating collaborative management as described in Table 2.2.

Table 2.2: Ten lessons for public managers undertaking collaborative management

	Lesson	Description
1	The network is not the only vehicle of collaborative management	Other vehicles include bilateral linkages and one-to-one relationships
2	Managers continue to do the bulk of their work within the hierarchy	Lateral connections overlie hierarchy rather than replace them; most time spent by managers is still working within the hierarchy (except for those with dedicated boundary spanning roles)
3	Network involvement brings several advantages that keep busy administrators involved	These include value added to individual managers especially in terms of learning; benefits accruing to the home agency such as resources, training and information; collective process skills and social capital; actual outputs and outcomes
4	Networks are different from organisations but not completely	They are different because they are non-hierarchical, require consensus seeking strategies and are multi-resourced; but are similar in that they require organisation, rules and operating systems
5	Not all networks make the types of policy and programme adjustments ascribed to them in the literature	There are four different types of networks – informational, developmental, outreach and action
6	Collaborative decisions or agreements are the products of a particular type of learning or adjustment	Networked decision making involves joint learning to create a collective power of new possibilities through e.g. group discussion, political negotiation
7	The most distinctive collaborative activity of all the networks proved to be their work in public sector knowledge management	Mixture of new explicit knowledge and the exchange of tacit knowledge
8	Despite the cooperative spirit and aura of accommodation in collaborative efforts, networks are not without conflict and power issues	Resulting from conflicts over agency turf, contribution of resources, staff time and frustration over time and effort; realisation that power is not equal

(continued)

Table 2.2: Ten lessons for public managers undertaking collaborative management (continued)

	Lesson	Description
9	Networks have their collaborative costs, as well as their benefits	Managers are concerned about giving up agency authority and turf resulting in loss of autonomy and control, loss of expertise and greater uncertainty
		Real costs include time/opportunity costs of network involvement; time/energy in decision-making processes; failure to reach agreements; gravitation towards consensus rather than risk strategies; resource hoarding
10	Networks alter the boundaries of the state only in the most marginal way; they do not appear to be replacing public bureaucracies in any way	Limits on the power of networks as much work continues to be undertaken in hierarchies particularly delivery and implementation; statutory and legal factors often constrain networks and favour individual agencies

Source: Adapted from Agranoff, 2006

Fountain (2013: 5), in a guide to help managers in the US Federal Government promote effective collaboration, concludes that collaboration is only sustainable if managers develop two types of practice as follows:

- **Collaboration through people**: Relationship skills must be developed for effective managers and teams. Team-building skills are those used by managers willing and able to work across jurisdictional boundaries to develop effective professional relationships and cohesive working groups. Skills needed by effective managers include active listening, fairness, and respect – qualities that produce trust in a cross-agency collaborative initiative. In cross-boundary teams, managers build informal relationships outside regular hierarchical channels. Teams function well when productive communities based on trust and professional experience form around a problem, project or practice.
- **Collaboration through processes**: In addition to effective managers and effective teams, cross-agency collaborative initiatives need effective organisational processes, which include a focus on strategy, operations, systems and their

management. Effective organisational processes demand an organisational skill set that emphasises rigour and clarity in setting goals, designing systems, building in milestones, attracting resources and framing an organisation that lies across agency boundaries.

A number of studies address the question about whether collaborative managers need to be of a particular type of person. Radin (1996) refers to studies that report on defined characteristics such as 'flexibility, extroversion, tolerance of ambiguity, self-assurance, need for visibility, and savior faire', and to this list adds 'personable, high achieving and verbal' from her research. Lank (2006: 128) compiles a pen picture of the personal qualities of the ideal perfect partner, and conversely the nightmare partner. She makes the point that 'these personal qualities are possibly more important considerations than subject matter expertise in many situations'.

The role of the 'global network manager' operating in multinational corporations offers an interesting perspective on collaborative managers in the private sector. Child (2006: 255) considers that these managers 'are the people between whom important communications flow; they consolidate information from various sources; they interpret and endeavour to reconcile corporate and local requirements; they act as a main point of transmission of information and policies to other parts and levels in the network'. He goes on to outline a number of distinct and demanding roles that they perform – boundary spanning between different levels and units; being initiators of networks by bringing together people who are dispersed geographically and organisationally; being coordinators, synthesisers and transferors of information; and being conveyors of corporate visions downward and advocates of decentralised initiatives upwards. Child (2006) tackles the question of the qualities needed to be an effective global network manager and these are listed in Box 2.2.

Box 2.2: Qualities of a global network manager

• Having a broad strategic awareness
• To be able to understand the nature of conflicting priorities and to handle their resolution within the network
• Ability to communicate effectively and flexibly
• Having personal skills of adaptability
• Ability to function in fluid conditions and cope with ambiguity and personal stress
• Relationship and negotiating skills
• Capacity to work with different groups
• High level of sensitivity to others especially those from different cultures
• Openness to learning from new situations and diverse points of view
• High levels of self-belief and self-reliance that fall short of personal arrogance
• The ability to manage people over whom they may have no direct authority

Source: Child, 2006

Role conflict is a source of concern for individuals involved in: 'juggling expectations from the interagency group or network and the "home base"' (Radin, 1996: 161). The tension between the 'gatekeeper' and 'representative' roles (Friedman and Podolny, 1992) can increase over time when the benefits of collaboration are tested and evaluated in practice. More fundamentally perhaps, are the stubborn and resistant problems associated with 'turf' protection – defined by Bardach (1996: 177) as 'the exclusive domain of activities and resources over which an agency has the right, or prerogative, to exercise operational and/or policy responsibility'. The size of a manager's 'turf' is a reflection of budget, number of staff and range of duties and responsibilities. It brings with it prestige, visibility and power, and loss of it can be perceived as a threat from a number of angles – threats to job security and career enhancement; challenges to professional expertise; conflict over physical facilities; loss of policy direction; undermining an agency's traditional priorities; anxiety over accountability; loss of self-worth; and problems associated with building and maintaining consensus. All of these, of course, are likely to be present in collaboration. Bardach (1996) suggests that middle managers tend to be less turf conscious than higher executives because of their dependency on the size, responsibilities and duties of their agency. However, this point is debatable because middle managers are similarly dependent in terms of their particular units and functions, and collaboration can equally be threatening. This may vary, of course, with some middle managers welcoming 'new, collaborative turf' and the potential it offers for innovation, creativity and working with others to tackle complex, social problems.

Leadership for collaboration

There is a substantial body of contested literature on the differences between management and leadership. Kotter (1990) takes the view that the core functions of modern management revolve around planning and budgeting, organising and staffing, and controlling and problem solving. In contrast, leadership is considered to be very different as it involves establishing direction, aligning people and motivating and inspiring. He argues that a fundamental difference relates to the primary function of each activity – leadership and management – the first offers the prospect of change, whereas the latter creates order and efficiency. Dickinson and Carey (2016: 22) summarise the literature on the subject in their conclusion that 'where leaders are transformational, managers are transactional' and 'the former do the right thing, while the latter merely do the thing right'. It is important not to conflate leadership with leaders and management with managers; a point underscored by Morse (2007: 4) in his comment that: 'certainly leaders must manage and managers must lead'. Leadership is not the unique domain of a privileged set of individuals with formal positions located at the apex of organisations. Other actors too, in this case middle managers, engage in leadership roles, functions and activities. The degree to which they discharge leadership functions varies widely depending on their particular roles, types of interventions and capabilities, but the implications of this point are profound, and consequently has the effect of widening any literature review to embrace leadership in collaboration. There is a growing consensus that collaborative leadership or inter-organisational leadership is significantly different in tone, style and approach and requires a different skill set and competence from that traditionally associated with intra-organisational leadership focused on leading within hierarchies. Crucially, it involves crossing a whole range of additional boundaries relating to sector, organisation, levels of governance and others. The problem for middle managers is that they are required to operate sometimes within hierarchies and, at other times, in collaboration – this can occur simultaneously and the boundaries can be unclear. There is a strong body of opinion that maintains that the competencies and behaviours required for leadership in collaboration are substantively different from those in hierarchies, while others argue that there are similarities between them, and at times intra-organisational leadership is appropriate for collaborative settings and vice versa. Unsurprisingly, the tensions, ambiguities and balances that middle managers have to make as a consequence, are both demanding and complex.

Soun Jang et al (2016: 8) argue that traditional hierarchical styles of leadership common in single agency bureaucracies are not appropriate to managing networks in non-hierarchical contexts, and that new leadership approaches are needed. They point to the importance of agency in collaboration and argue that:

> Different styles of leadership will show different activities that either enhance or reduce effective collaborations. This is because a public manager who leads a collaborative network plays an incredibly important role in the process. Among other responsibilities, they are commonly tasked with bringing organisations together to participate, securing the necessary resources to achieve the goals of the network, and articulating a common vision and mission. Scholarly research has usually treated network leaders as agents of underlying organisational

decisions driving the management of collaborations. But public managers leading collaborative efforts are real people who possess leadership qualities and skills that will influence effective collaboration in predictable ways.

Soun Jong et al's research on homeless networks suggest that effective leadership comprises two interrelated types of behaviour:

- task-orientated behaviours – reflecting four essential tasks of network activation, mobilisation, framing and synthesising;
- relationship orientated behaviours – that 'place a greater focus on building positive social relations, such as motivating and inspiring network members and ensuring that the individual needs of members are carefully addressed' (p. 14) and creating a culture that stimulates innovation and creativity.

The literature on leadership within organisations is voluminous and diverse (Palmer and Hardy, 2000; Parry and Bryman, 2006), represented by many different models and theories based on trait, style, contingency, new leadership (transactional, transformational, charismatic, visionary), that are distributed and collaborative. Many of these are accompanied by the skills, abilities, attributes, competencies and behaviours required by managers and leaders to be effective, that are particularly useful for informing the design and delivery of education, training and development programmes. Typically, the new leadership and collaborative leadership models move away from the notion of the 'heroic' leader sitting at the top of organisations and directing the 'followers' in a largely unidirectional and hierarchical manner, to forms that embrace other stakeholders and interests in the process from all levels in an organisation and externally.

The literature on leadership for collaboration, while relatively recent compared to that within organisations, has steadily grown in extent and insight, particularly in response to collaborative forms of working across the breadth of public policy. A number of models have now been advanced that emphasise sharing power, distributing responsibilities, inclusivity, building coalitions and mutual learning (Crosby and Bryson, 2005; Chrislip and Larson, 1994; Alexander et al, 2001; Linden, 2010; Luke, 1998). Middle managers intent on practising effective leadership for collaboration would need to demonstrate a number of key skills and capabilities as follows:

- having the inter-personal skills to build and sustain relationships between diverse stakeholders, and to promote inclusive processes particularly in groups and networks;
- appreciating complexity and connectivity between interdependent policy systems and environments over time, space and function – this being a job for 'clever people' and 'deep thinkers' (Kanter, 1997);
- performing as translators by understanding the diverse meanings and aspirations of disparate constituencies – the agencies, professions, cultures and sectors involved in collaborative endeavours;
- being creative with the ability to promote innovation, experimentation and cross fertilisation of ideas and practices;
- promoting a learning environment to reflect the emergent and complex nature of the prevailing environment, and to promote reflection, conceptualisation and thinking among the participants;
- being committed to dispersed, shared and distributed forms of leadership through empowerment strategies and decision-making processes that encourage accountability and responsibility within collaborative settings.

Sullivan et al's (2012b) conceptualisation of leadership for collaboration as situated agency in practice, also emphasises many of these characteristics – co-governing through inclusive relationships; co-governing through expert facilitation; negotiating dynamic complexity; judicious use of elites; and the attainment of key outcomes.

These leadership characteristics and approaches have been used as the basis for the identification of associated competencies and attributes. For example, Morse (2007) generates a framework of collaborative leadership competencies as illustrated in Table 2.3. He considers that these competencies are additional to those

Table 2.3: Collaborative leadership competencies

Personal attributes	Skills	Behaviours
• Collaborative mindset • Passion towards outcomes • Systems thinking • Openness and risk taking • Mutuality and connectedness • Humility	• Self-management • Strategic skills • Facilitation skills	• Stakeholder identification and assessment • Strategic issue framing • Relationship development with key stakeholders • Convening working groups • Facilitating mutual learning processes • Inducing commitment Facilitating trusting relationships among partners

Source: Morse, 2007

considered by van Wart (2003) to be essential for leadership within organisations.

In terms of general style, collaborative leadership espouses the virtues of advocacy and facilitation that are considered to be characteristically different from 'the normal "top-down" ones that dominate discussions of organisational leadership' (Morse, 2007: 12). A number of interesting questions flow from this discussion including, whether it is possible or appropriate to change styles seamlessly to fit the context, or whether a manager has to adopt one default approach? It may be that leadership for collaboration cannot be divorced from organisational and personal leadership, and that the different levels of leadership impact on one another. For instance, it has been observed that organisations that tend to work together well in collaboration, are ones that have internal working cultures that emphasise cross-departmental and joint working. Also, there is an interesting argument that suggests that while it may be possible to learn the skills of collaborative leadership, if this is not underpinned by an accompanying collaborative mindset, it will ultimately fail to be effective because of its lack of authenticity. Box 2.3 presents a profile of a collaborative leader prepared by the National Academy of Public Administration (2007) that clearly highlights the values, principles and mindset considered fundamental to working in a collaborative context. These relate to personal behaviour and relationships with others. It also makes the point that collaborative leaders are developed and not born, but the ability to alter a value system developed over time, grounded in a particular family and social background, and tempered by education and professional training, is often difficult to overcome.

Box 2.3. Profile of a collaborative leader

Collaborative leaders exhibit a mindset. They demonstrate values and assumptions that drive collaborative behaviour and use of a collaborative problem-solving process that leads to outcomes that are different and better than any party envisioned when they began to address the problem. The behaviours of a collaborative leader include:

- authenticity;
- an ability to be aware of one's own strengths and weaknesses;
- an understanding of the impact of behaviour on others;
- the ability to identify core values, identity, emotions, motives and goals;
- the willingness to be relationally transparent by sharing their core feelings, motives, and inclinations with others, and showing both positive and negative aspects of themselves to others;
- compassion;
- curiosity;
- the willingness to hold oneself accountable for one's behaviour rather than blaming others;
- a focus on creating the trust necessary for the participants to feel sufficiently safe to offer their ideas, insights, and possible solutions into the mix.

A collaborative leader is willing to use an interest-based problem-solving process to stimulate the identification of interests, which creates a broader base for reaching resolution rather than fighting narrowly over positions and creating winners and losers. A collaborative leader recognises that it may take longer to reach a decision using an interest-based problem-solving process, but implementation is faster because the interests of all parties have been met, and all parties are collaborating to implement the final decision. Collaborative leaders are not born, they are developed.

Source: National Academy of Public Administration, 2007: 143

This chapter is intended as a backcloth for a subsequent exploration of the role and behaviours of middle managers working in collaboration. It has looked at the changing nature of public management before delving more closely into the organisational lives of public managers – especially middle managers. It moved on to examine the nature and context of collaboration, highlighting its particular characteristics and diverse forms. Finally, the discussion progressed to consider different approaches to management in collaboration, and the notion of the 'collaborative manager' in this form of governance.

Key points of learning

- The design and delivery of public policy and management have been grounded in a **number of dominant theoretical models** – Public Administration, New Public Management and New Public Governance – but in practice differences between these approaches can be confused.
- **Public Administration** focuses on public service delivery prescribed by legislation, with public administrators governed by rules and procedures; whereas public management is driven more by public purposes and the process of strategic choice, and management viewed as a craft and the product of actions and decisions of public managers; **New Public Management** is influenced by the businesslike practices of the private sector and emphasises efficiency and performance; and **New Public Governance** approaches reflect the preponderance of cross-cutting issues and the need to develop interorganisational relationships and collaborative governance frameworks of decision making.
- These **different management models suggest the need for different management skills and approaches**. Van

der Wal (2017) characterises three types of public manager based on these models – the traditional, rule-orientated bureaucrat operating within a hierarchical, formalised and bureaucratic organisation with authority based on expertise and knowledge; the 'businesslike', performance-focused manager responding to the demands of New Public Management and embracing values of efficiency, value for money, market mechanisms and outsourcing; and the networking, relation-focused collaborator who works with others to tackle cross-boundary issues and problems.

• Various perspectives are advanced on the role and behaviours of '**middle managers**'. Fulop and Linstead (2004) identify four key roles undertaken – creators and implementers of strategy; influencers because of their juxtaposition between vertical and horizontal communication; key sources of stability perhaps even resistance to change but certainly as a consolidator of change; and drivers of continual change; Haneberg (2010) suggests that a middle manager's role includes a diverse range of tasks including planning, performance management, problem solving, communication and budgeting; Floyd and Wooldridge (1994) see middle managers as part of an organisation's control system, particularly translating strategies defined at higher levels into actions at operating levels involving budgeting and human resource management; and Spreitzer and Quinn (1996) argue that traditional middle managers' roles must change from being transactional to transformational in character.

• Collaboration has revolutionised approaches to the design and delivery of public services. It is a **highly contested term** with accompanying theoretical literature that is both diverse and interdisciplinary. A collaborative context consists of a number of components that are influential and instrumental in shaping effective management approaches and behaviours, and these relate to motivation, purpose and objectives, power relationships, culture, values and ways of working, legal and financial frameworks, and accountability and performance.

• Some researchers detect a **basic difference between managing in hierarchies and managing in collaboration**. Approaches to managing in collaboration include network management and collaborative public management involving different roles, skills and behaviours.

- **Perspectives on the collaborative manager** include the work of Williams (2002 and 2012) on boundary spanners who discharge a number of key roles – reticulist, interpreter/ communicator, coordinator and entrepreneur – with a high degree of interplay and connectivity between them, and each demanding a particular set of skills and competencies; the six categories of professional skills for collaborative governance (Donahue, 2004; O'Leary and Gerard's (2012) skill set of a successful collaborator consisting of individual attributes, interpersonal skills, group process skills, strategic leadership and substantive/technical expertise; Agranoff's (2006) ten lessons for public managers contemplating collaborative management; and Child's (2006) qualities of an effective global network manager.

- Accepting the argument that middle managers engage in various leadership roles, functions and activities, the literature on **leadership in collaboration** suggests that they need to have interpersonal skills to build and sustain relationships between diverse stakeholders, and to promote inclusive processes particularly in groups and networks; to appreciate complexity and interdependency; to act as translators by understanding the diverse meanings and aspirations of different actors; to demonstrate creativity, innovation and entrepreneurship; to promote a learning environment; and to practise dispersed, shared and distributed forms of leadership.

Suggested further reading

6, P., Goodwin, N., Peck, E. and Freeman, T. (2006) *Managing Networks of Twenty-first Century Organisations*, Basingstoke: Palgrave

Agranoff, R. (2012) *Collaborating to Manage: A Primer for the Public Sector*, Washington, DC: Georgetown University Press

Bardach, E. (1996) 'Turf barriers to interagency collaboration', in D.F. Kettl and H.B. Milward (eds) *The State of Public Management*, Baltimore, MD and London: John Hopkins University Press

Herranz, J. (2008) 'The multisectoral trilemma of network management', *Journal of Public Administration Research and Theory*, Vol. 18 (1), pp. 1–31

O'Flynn, J., Blackman, D. and Halligan, J. (2014) *Crossing Boundaries in Public Management and Policy: The International Experience*, London: Routledge

O'Leary, R. and Bingham, L.B. (2009) *The Collaborative Public Manager: New Ideas for the Twenty-First Century*, Washington, DC: Georgetown University Press

Popp, J.K., Milward, H.B., MacKean, G., Casebeer, A. and Lindstrom, R. (2014) *Inter-Organisational Networks: A Review of the Literature to Inform Practice*, Washington, DC: The IBM Center for the Business of Government

Sandfort, J. and Milward, H.B. (2008) 'Collaborative service provision in the public sector', in S. Cropper, M. Ebers, C. Huxham and P. Smith Ring (eds) *The Oxford Handbook of Inter-Organisational Relations*, Oxford: Oxford University Press

van der Wal, Z. (2017) *The 21st Century Public Manager*, London: Palgrave

van Meerkerk, I. and Edelenbos, J. (2018) *Boundary Spanners in Public Management and Governance: An Interdisciplinary Assessment*, London: Edward Elgar

Williams, P. (2002) 'The competent boundary spanner', *Public Administration*, Vol. 80 (1), pp. 103–124

3

Managing for common purpose

"There is always a bit of 'giving your own kids away' in collaboration and a consequent feeling of loss of control and power." (Local Council manager)

The very essence of collaboration lies in the quest for common purpose among participating actors and organisations. Without such an understanding, this type of endeavour is doomed to failure. It is critical, therefore, for middle managers who are engaged in this form of working, to fully appreciate what is involved in 'managing for common purpose', what form it takes, and how it can be developed and sustained at different levels – personal, professional, organisational and sectoral.

Understanding what might constitute 'common purpose' derives from the diverse motivations underpinning the drive to collaboration. These can broadly be grouped under three forms – efficiency, effectiveness and responsiveness. The efficiency discourse relates to the need to make the best use of limited resources – particularly financial – and is especially prominent in the austere times of countries such as the UK over recent years. Local councils in England, for instance, have had their budgets reduced by roughly 25 per cent between 2010 and 2017. Other public authorities such as the NHS have experienced equally challenging financial difficulties – exacerbated by the ever-rising demands upon its services. It would appear a 'no-brainer' to many, that such a situation would be a catalyst for agencies looking for ways in which they might pool/share/combine their resources to make the most efficient use of them – especially when they often serve the same clients and operate in matching geographical areas. Countless examples of this happening can be evidenced, but the downward financial pressure on some organisations is not always a fillip to collaboration. Paradoxically, the reverse can occur where managers and organisations consider that working in collaboration is too risky and time consuming with outcomes that are not guaranteed. So, rather than providing a stimulation to collaboration – ever increasing financial pressures can result in a withdrawal from existing initiatives and a reluctance to venture into new ones. This can be underpinned by a need for some authorities to seek to fulfil at all costs their statutory duties in relation to particular services. Failure to deliver on these can be a source of embarrassment and legal risk.

The effect of the 'age of austerity' discourse – 'do more with less' and 'we are all in this together' is exemplified in a case study involving 'integration' of health and social care services in one area. As a driver for enhanced integration, one consequence of this narrative is that integration should be viewed as a source of institutional entrepreneurship (Lawrence et al, 2002) resulting in moves, for example, between local authorities to develop shared services, community budgets, joint appointments, joint working arrangements, merged departments, joint procurement, and commissioning of services from the private sector and new social enterprises. This position was articulated by a middle manager in one research study (Williams, 2013a) in the following terms:

> "in an age of austerity, it is the accountants and treasurers who become the life-blood of an organisation – but these are risk averse in the way in which they manage money – the focus is on these people who are least likely to move the organisation out of this territory – this is difficult to arrest in high profile times when there are acute issues of accountability – the focus should be on innovation and looking for new ways of delivery services – not cutting and scything."

Lowndes and Squires (2012: 408) suggest that: 'partnerships have the potential to 'buffer' communities from the effects of spending cuts and recession, through making better use of existing resources and generating entirely novel insights and capacities'. Certainly, for some interviewees in the research study, the dire economic circumstances were considered as a rationale for more effective integration including a focus on innovation and creativity in service development and delivery. Conversely, for managers and their agencies that perceived collaboration as a 'bolt-on' to mainstream organisational activities and a considerable drain in terms of time and resources for questionable rewards, continued integration was not justified. The view here was that organisations should default back to their separate statutory roles and responsibilities to ensure that there was clarity in terms of being held to public account through individual performance management frameworks and systems of oversight. One middle manager commented that:

> "we did more joint working with the locality authority five years ago – but now with austerity measures, cuts in services and staff moving, people are far busier and more focused on their own agendas – we all have withdrawn and this is perpetuated by being in separate organisations – the agenda pulls us apart rather than together."

A third position articulated by some in the research study was that the narrative of the 'age of austerity' merely reinforced an existing imperative that concerned the necessity for a major re-configuration of health services from secondary to primary levels. In that sense it served to provide an extra legitimacy and immediacy to an existing policy direction.

A second dominant discourse underpinning the drive to collaboration relates to effectiveness and is premised on the notion and character of 'wicked issues' – socially constructed, multiply framed, resistant to optimal solutions and spilling across different types of boundary – compelling reasons for managers and organisations to work together to plan and deliver policies and interventions. Arguably, the long and ever-increasing list of 'wicked issues' facing public authorities from climate change to anti-social behaviour can sometimes render the notion somewhat vacuous, but there is little doubting its general thrust. The main problem occurs when every problem or issue is considered to be 'wicked' rather than a more nuanced view that judges many to still be amenable for management by single organisations. Identifying and negotiating common purpose among a range of actors and organisations involved in the management of a 'wicked issue' is particularly complex. Responsiveness – the third dominant collaborative discourse – is a more recent addition to the public policy scene and reflects a view that the design and delivery of public services should not be the exclusive domain of providers and government, but should be undertaken in concert with the recipients of those services. This adds many layers of complexity to managing in collaboration – some relate to the nature of the power relationships of the actors involved, and others to defining the status of the recipients of services – clients, customers, residents, voters – and to the methodologies for involving them in policymaking processes.

One important aspect of collaboration and its underlying motivations relate to whether it is voluntary or mandated. There has been an increasing tendency in the UK for government, partly in a response to a perceived frustration of a failure by some public bodies to embrace collaboration, to force collaboration through statutory duties. This might be helpful in some circumstances where existing legislation is a barrier to collaboration, and where system-wide leadership might provoke action, but enforced collaboration is inherently fraught with difficulties. There is a limit to what statutory duties can prescribe in practice – for instance, what does collaboration or working in partnership actually mean – and unless participating actors fully understand and appreciate the value to them and their organisation of this mode of governance, there are likely to be many limitations to this approach. Mandated collaboration should be used sparingly and sensitively. It should be used to remove barriers and blockages and catalyse collaboration rather than force actors and organisations together against their wills and better judgement.

There are a number of interesting aspects to these collaborative discourses that need to be taken into account when designing policy and practice:

1. Individual discourses tend to be sponsored and championed by particular actors and organisations. For instance, the efficiency discourse is typically associated with managers from finance and accounting backgrounds; whereas the responsiveness discourse is favoured by managers dealing with services with particularly close links to service users such as in health, social care and community regeneration.

2. Different discourses gain prominence and traction at particular periods; they are dynamic and can alter over time. The prevailing 'age of austerity' is fuelling the efficiency discourse, and the dominance of professionalism is being challenged by views that advocate a participatory role for service users in public service design and delivery.

3. What is important is that it is commonplace for managers involved in a collaboration to project and support different collaborative discourses. Differences in fundamental motivations to collaborate make the subsequent process of working together more difficult, and how this is tackled in practice is a matter of debate. An obvious approach is one that encourages 'openness' and 'honesty' from the various actors, providing the basis for everyone to appreciate the total amalgam of individual views, ambitions and problems, and providing the basis upon which consensus and common purpose might be negotiated. However, such a degree of openness might lead to the surfacing of a range of intractable conflicts that risk paralysing the collaborative process and render it ineffective. Arguably, an alternative approach might aim to pursue a more incremental process based on not totally 'outing' a person's motivations but on identifying areas of agreement that are sufficient to move the collaboration forward. This might give confidence to participants that the process of collaboration is worthwhile and encourage further interactions, and the tackling of more difficult areas of disagreement. This general approach does risk potential difficulties in circumstances where outcomes are not those originally envisaged, because motivations and objectives were suppressed. It goes without saying that the ability to unpick, appreciate, influence and manage within

this mosaic of relationships is an exceptionally valuable skill of a middle manager.

Understanding and negotiating common purpose

The key importance of achieving common purpose between participating actors and agencies is underscored in the following:

> To overcome significant differences in agency missions, cultures, and established ways of doing business, collaborating agencies must have a clear and compelling rationale to work together. The compelling rationale for agencies to collaborate can be imposed externally through legislation or other directives or can come from the agencies' own perceptions of the benefits they can obtain from working together. In either case, the collaborative effort requires agency staff working across agency lines to define and articulate the common federal outcome or purpose they are seeking to achieve that is consistent with their respective agency goals and mission. Moreover, the development of a common outcome takes place over time and requires sustained resources and commitment. (GAO, 2005: 11)

It appears that the answer lies in devising a form of common purpose that is consistent with each of the 'self-interests' of the participating organisations. The usual manner in which this is attempted in a formal sense is through various mechanisms such as visions, missions, value statements and core purpose statements, further articulated through frameworks of goals, aims and objectives. The first observation to make is that a trawl through many such exercises reveals a high degree of unnecessary complexity, repetition and lack of coherence. In an effort to appease all parties, there is a danger of including too much rather than concentrating on the areas where the value of collaboration is best captured – less is more! The use of 'visions' and 'missions' can often result in amorphous and meaningless statements. 'Visions' have a ring of biblical connotation about them, and perhaps would be better termed 'envisions' to capture a desired future state or outcome that can be manufactured rather than prayed for! Undoubtedly, a well-crafted vision or mission can be a catalyst for action and experience suggests that they should be tested against a number of criteria – credibility, ownership, achievability and uniqueness.

Credibility relates to whether the outcomes and purposes set out are believable by both providers and recipients of the services and policies – 'motherhood and apple-pie' statements should be avoided at all costs; achievable in the sense that the desired outcomes are not overly-ambitious and unrealistic; unique to the particular collaborative concerned; and perhaps above all, owned by the actors and organisations that design them. An important lesson here is to ensure that there is not a detachment between the designers and the implementers (and recipients of the services/policies) in the crafting of common purpose. The practice of senior managers, predominantly at the apex of organisations, getting together, bonding and producing purpose statements, which they then attempt to sell to the rest of their organisations, is not tenable. Ownership is more likely to be propagated through equal participation from all levels in the hierarchy, and critically, it is important that there is not an artificial separation between the planners and implementers of the collaborative policymaking process. This reinforces the views of Currie and Procter (2005) and Floyd and Wooldridge (1997) discussed in the previous chapter.

Uhl-Bien and Marion (2009) make an interesting point in relation to negotiating common purpose when they claim that there is a clear distinction between shared need and shared goal or vision. They state that shared need: 'does not require agents to hold the same goal or vision. Rather, it recognises that in collaborative efforts, partners often do not share the exact same goals but instead have personal needs that can best be satisfied by working together'. In other words, shared need recognises interdependence, and the practical implications for management and leadership are that:

> focusing attention on getting alignment around a shared vision or goal may be a waste of time or even

undesirable (it may dampen creativity by fostering homogeneity over heterogeneity). It suggests that interdependence is a more powerful force for change than alignment around a 'single' vision (or shared goal). The implication of shared vision suggests, 'changing' someone's needs to match the leader's vision – a task that becomes quite lofty, and often unattainable, in reality. Shared need instead starts with the 'what's in it for me?' question and whether it is advantageous to work together to accomplish personal goals; it understands that if interdependence is not inherent or acknowledged, the likelihood of fully engaging others is slim. (Uhl-Bien and Marion, 2009: 642)

The key message for both managers and leaders is that to enable collaborative behaviours to prosper, they need to create the conditions to promote interdependencies among actors in the system, not artificial interdependencies, but ones where actors perceive clear connections that are sufficient to mobilise them to work with others.

One example of common purpose is expressed in a project in Wales that is designed to deliver integrated health and social care services. Here, managers considered that it was important to have a vision and an accompanying set of principles to provide the strategic direction. The nature of the vision – 'making a difference to the lives of vulnerable people' was considered to be both 'deserving' and 'socially just' and appealed to managers and professionals who were motivated both by public service values and to improving the quality of life of individuals and communities. The nature of this vision and its wording – embracing a desire to re-balance care for people between a hospital environment and their homes to be more in favour of the latter – allowed different agencies to offer their commitment at a strategic level without too much conflict at the early stages of a multi-agency initiative. The vision could be operationalised in a flexible manner in response to emerging and changing political priorities, resources and local circumstances.

Another key message in the effective crafting and delivery of common purpose concerns the need to ensure that there are clear mechanisms in place to judge the extent to which these have been achieved. There needs to be a coherent and integrated framework to measure outcomes and assess performance along the journey. Furthermore, this matter needs to be incorporated into the policymaking process from its initiation and not considered as an afterthought. The matter of assessing and measuring outcomes and performance is notoriously difficult even within single agencies, but in collaboration, it increases to new levels of complexity in many aspects – theoretically, methodologically and practically. These, however, cannot be ducked in a policy environment that craves 'what works' and 'evidence based-policymaking'. An interesting perspective on the importance of evaluation is provided by one collaborative project (Pathways to Work: Condition Management Programme). Here, evaluation was partly evidenced through customer feedback and the 'stories' of people whose lives had been improved as a result of participating in the project. The effect of this 'success' and the 'powerful boost of patient stories' was considered to provide a great fillip to the managers working on the project and reinforced their commitment to achieving the project's aims. In the words of one manager: "All those tears and tantrums and difficult discussions have been worth it – the stories are so emotional about people's life-changes."

Box 3.1: Case study on managing for outcomes

A highly instructive case study reflects the efforts made by New Zealand government over a five-year period to measure its efforts to address societal problems spanning traditional agency boundaries (Scott and Boyd, 2017). Initially, a framework referred to as 'Managing for Outcomes' involving clusters of agencies measuring their collective impact was introduced, and this was shortly followed by a sectoral approach with different sectors responsible for developing overlapping outcomes. Both regimes were eventually replaced by a system of interagency performance targets. Following an evaluation of the design and use of this system, a number of lessons for policy makers and practitioners have been established:

- *Selecting results:* focus on a few problems; involve other agencies in selecting problems to be addressed; build on existing relationships when selecting results to pursue; measure intermediate outcomes; align results, targets and measures; commit publicly.
- *Developing accountability:* hold leaders collectively responsible; get started and learn by doing.
- *Measuring collaboration:* start simply; limit group size; signal shared responsibility.
- *Reporting on progress:* report on trends; share success stories.

Perspectives from middle managers

The question of crafting and negotiating common purpose was explored in a study of middle managers employed in a Welsh local authority, involving a variety of collaborative endeavours with other pubwlic, private and third sector partners. There was broad agreement that effective collaboration was conditional on there being agreement on a common purpose. Clarity was seen as particularly important to ensure that the combined efforts and resources of the different agencies were channelled in a mutually agreed direction to secure jointly agreed outcomes. The following extracts from a number of interviewees' gives a flavour of the middle managers' opinions on this matter (Box 3.2).

Box 3.2: Views on negotiating common purpose

- "Understanding other people's priorities" is a prerequisite of negotiating common purpose, and "it is important to understand the competing demands between an individual organisation and those of a collaboration – there is a need for regular communication to appreciate others' difficulties – and that I make myself available to attend others' meetings."
- "There is a need to encourage openness – asking for explanation and clarification and being facilitative, a good listener and approachable."

- "There is a need to give and take because we all share a common goal, that collaboration is the only way to go and that we are all in it together."
- "It was necessary to have a good grasp of our own organisational issues – to understand other people's interests and to boil them down into a consensus – to look at the different contributions from each and to help the more reluctant partners understand their interests and contributions."
- "Listening and taking into account the impact on other people" – "having empathy and putting yourself in their position – negotiating for the benefit of both parties."
- "Must appreciate other people's difficulties – the political parameters in which they work – having the empathy to understand where they are coming from."
- "Being supportive – can't dictate to others – must bend for different people to get it to work – process is slow because you have to work in different ways."

Source: Williams, 2013b

Understanding the perspectives of other partners – what drives them, what they are trying to achieve, and what difficulties they face, whether professional, organisational, statutory or other, were considered to be a highly prized competency. The importance of seeing the world through the eyes of partners was seen as fundamental to collaborative negotiations in order to get a handle on partner's flexibilities and 'red lines'. The processes involved here are those referred to as 'framing', which actors use to make sense of reality – in this context, the world of collaboration. Frames are used as cognitive lenses to help conceptualise and understand realities (Benford and Snow, 2000), and critically, are a reflection of an individual actors' background – social, professional and organisational. They may be influenced by values and attitudes, and they function as a means of understanding the nature of public problems, their causes and potential solutions. De Leeuw and Browne (2018: 538) go as far as to maintain that: 'the art of mastering discourse, framing and storytelling may well be key to successfully bridging the nexus between whatever is construed as "the evidence" and the negotiated endeavour to resolve social problems (that is, "policy")'. Unsurprisingly, middle managers engaged in collaborative action bring with them a diversity of frames, which can result in conflict and dilemmas. In many ways, the core task of a collaboration is to attempt to agree or stamp a common frame, which may involve choosing between an existing one or restructuring and devising a new one. As the interviewees suggest above, it is important to identify and seek clarity about individual 'frames' to help identify potential areas of consensus, conflict and interdependency, and offer the basis upon which negotiated collaborative solutions can be forged. This general point about trying to understand the world through the lenses of partners was emphasised by a research interviewee in his reflections about the difficulties of managing in collaboration. He commented that:

> "we talk slightly different languages and are the subject of different policies and rules – we interpret things differently because of organisational restrictions. This is compounded by images of professionalism – professionals are exposed and uncomfortable to challenge and to admit they don't know – they often resort to jargon in an effort to obfuscate – but I'm not afraid of looking daft."

Another middle manager concurred with the need to: "being able to admit ignorance", although acknowledging that this can be difficult for some whose very professionalism is grounded in a belief that they know what's best and of being fountains of all knowledge in their particular specialist areas.

Types of 'frames' vary widely. At a macro level, there was frequent reference to the notion of 'the greater good' in the research referred to above which was about negotiating shared purposes between the different self-interests of the various individual and organisational interests involved, and providing the basis upon which effective collaborations could be developed and sustained. Others relate to the underlying motivations to collaborate – efficiency, effectiveness or responsiveness. Different professional groups have different notions of how the recipients of their services should be involved in the policymaking process, and the value base of public services often collide between the public, private and third sectors. The recent history of public–private finance initiatives in UK public services is a case study on the underlying tensions between public and private interests that have surfaced and caused much political acrimony. One example of the process of framing can be illustrated through the different 'understandings' of the notion of a locality model in the design and delivery of health and social care in Wrexham, North Wales. Box 3.3 catalogues the different views of middle managers on this model.

Box 3.3: Framing the locality model

- "It is a delivery mechanism based on geography and population size – it focuses services around a certain population that enables health providers to deliver population-sensitive services and to deliver and link different models of care that are sensitive to the needs of that population."
- "It means different things to different people – to me it is about the efficient and effective use of services and a vehicle to deliver the chronic condition management agenda – but, it can be used to deliver other health and social care outcomes."
- "It is a multi-disciplinary team within a geographically defined area linked to a number of general practitioner practices."
- "It's about fewer people in hospital beds and keeping more people at home, and a greater involvement of social services."
- "A method by which smaller populations can have local needs developed for them – a framework for delivering a whole range of imperatives."
- "It's getting a balance between economies of scale, but being not too big as to not have a local feel – efficient and effective use of services but with a user focus which allows their ownership and involvement."
- "Getting the best use of resources in a particular area but also about the community in that area."
- "To coordinate the management arrangements and resources in one locality – to create an alignment between people serving the same

population through effective clinical and managerial leadership resulting in a re-shaping in the use of resources."
• "Coordinating management arrangements and resources in one locality."
• "It's a framework for organising and delivering some health services at a community level (for example, district nurses, community nurses and school nurses in integrated teams), primary care services through GPs, and selective secondary care services related to chronic condition management (for example, end of life, primary mental health, virtual clinics)."

This one model thus embraces a whole gamut of frames – efficiency, effectiveness, responsiveness, coordination and a management tool – summed up by one manager as "it means different things to different people". In practice, and given the variety of understandings of this model and expectations that ranged from modest to more radical expressions such as 'area budgeting' and 'joint commissioning', the local partnership group attempted to operationalise the model through an incremental and emergent approach rather than an overly planned strategy – described by one middle manager as "shapes forming in the mist". Broadly, the methodology involved the identification, exploration and testing of various projects, with an emphasis on innovation and joint learning – "it's exploratory, a loose framework, about networking and bringing people together to see what emerges".

Another example of framing is frequently demonstrated in understandings of the notion of 'integration' – a highly contested term attracting multiple interpretations and meanings (Kodner and Spreeuwenberg, 2002; Williams and Sullivan, 2009). These can be arrayed along a continuum from relatively weak forms of relationships that revolve around sharing information and some joint working, through to more mature forms of coordination and service planning, but with governance and accountability still divided, and ultimately to a fully merged and unified health and social care organisation (Gajda, 2004). Expressions of integration can be gauged in relation to co-location of services, models of care, common assessment frameworks, budget arrangements, multi-disciplinary working, performance management systems, unified leadership and management structures and common information systems, protocols and policies. The example highlighted in Box 3.4 shows how a focus on a negotiated shared purpose between different interests can be the catalyst for a new model of service delivery for a vulnerable group of service users.

Box 3.4: Shared purpose: Mental Health Assisted Recovery Scheme

The value of shared purpose is demonstrated in the context of a Mental Health Assisted Recovery Scheme – an integrated health and social care service bringing together managers from a local health authority, local council and voluntary sector. The previously fragmented service needed to be grounded in a fundamentally new service model that was designed and owned by all stakeholders. In this case, a 'recovery model' was developed, which embraced the principles of user empowerment, personalised care, and planning and delivery within the community. This was a radical departure from the previous paternalistic, overly dependent, inflexible, group-focused, day care services offered in a residential setting. The significance of this new service model was its potential for being able to cross boundaries, and to channel effort towards a common purpose, overriding narrow organisational, sectional and professional interests. It provided a mechanism for negotiating new models of practice that moved away from stereotypic ones based on medical or social models of health underpinned by 'discipline-based visions of clientele' (D'Amour and Oandasan, 2005); and it was frequently deployed as a rallying call and source of motivation, particularly in times of conflict and disagreement.

Source: Williams, 2012b

The practical implications on the ground of the different interpretations of 'integration' are demonstrated in a case study in South Wales involving a health and social care partnership. Research evidence reported that: "it means different things to different people" – with some interests clearly aspiring to the ultimate goal of a fully merged health and social care service ("unified responsibilities and budgets is the way to go" and "the gold standard is a single organisation"), and others, especially in the local authority who feared being 'swallowed up' by health ("we are the minnows"), and content to preserve the autonomy of two agencies, but with more effective coordinating arrangements. This confusion was compounded by the problems of determining the merits of different models of integration and the lack of a robust evidence-base, with critics of fully developed forms of integration complaining that their justification was often based on empty rhetoric and blind faith. The research study also suggested that some managers involved claimed that the local health and social care system lacked a common vision or plan. One manager stated that: "I don't have a vision for a fully integrated service – I have no appetite for it – I'm not convinced it's the best solution and it will be too costly to dismantle two existing structures – my preference is to look for pragmatic, process-wide improvements based on relationships rather than structures." This view was reinforced by another interviewee who referred to there being: "no end game – just a process of incremental developments – based on what works on the ground and seeing what happened". Alternatively, another manager stated that: "it was inevitable that there would be a merger between health and social care". One manager reflected that model of integration should be about: "coordination of the respective contributions and roles of different professionals". The prospect of a single organisation for health and social care was seen as being: "a million miles away". A similar situation was apparent from the initial evaluation of an integrated heath and social care facility (Monnow Vale, South Wales). Although there was high level consensus on integration as a vehicle to 'provide seamless services', 'to be user-focused', 'to focus on patient pathways rather than institutional convenience', operationalising the notion uncovered significant views. For instance, there is often a tendency to conflate 'coordination' with 'integration' whereas as one manager explained: "a key worker can undertake coordination for a patient but integration involves bringing teams and resources together, making the best use of resources, removing duplication and working to a joint set of objectives and common purpose". Acknowledging the different interpretations of 'integration', in practice, the approach to operationalising this model in this project was emergent and pragmatic with change constantly being negotiated between key stakeholders.

The elasticity in the notion of 'integration' resonates closely with what Smith (2013) refers to as 'chameleonic ideas'. The characteristics of this type of idea are that they are inherently vague and are able to be transformable as they move between different actors and contexts. The idea encapsulates multiple meanings that allow them to be translated into different policy contexts to fit into prevailing discourses and policy environments; they can survive because they can be interpreted in situations even populated by opposing interests. Equality and sustainable development have similarly chameleonic qualities. The processes of frame articulation and understanding are not straightforward, and some managers are able to function as managers of meaning or 'frame articulators' to help others with their individual interpretations. This is a potentially highly influential skill because there are clear relationships between particular frames and interests, and also, frames are not static but dynamic and susceptible to the fluctuations in the public policy arena. Changes in government, emerging social and economic pressures, research evaluations and new innovations all help to influence and stimulate prevailing and future framing processes. The importance of framing is also underscored in the seminal work of Kingdon (1984) on 'policy entrepreneurs' – 'the agents for policy change who possess the knowledge, power, tenacity and luck to be able to exploit key opportunities' (Cairney, 2018: 201) through strategies based on agenda-setting, timing and responding/creating windows of opportunity. In particular, Cairney (2018: 211) argues that such agents: 'tell a persuasive story to frame a policy problem' and 'reinforce the cognitive biases of influential policy makers by combining facts with values and emotional appeals, and by framing policy solutions as consistent with dominant ways to understand problems'. This is a really important skill in collaborative arenas where actors are bombarded with highly complex and contested information and data from a wide variety of sources. The ability of a middle manager working in collaboration to discharge this framing role – coupled with the other elements of Kingdon's model relating to having ready-made solutions available, and being responsive and adaptable to the windows of opportunity, is highly influential.

Key points of learning

- **Common purpose** defines the very essence of collaboration and middle managers need to appreciate what form it takes, and how it can be developed and sustained at different levels – organisational and sectoral – and between different actors – personal, professional and service users.
- **Three broad types of motivation or discourse** – efficiency, effectiveness and responsiveness – significantly influence the understanding of common purpose; individual discourses are supported by particular actors and organisations; different discourses gain prominence and traction at particular times, and they can be imposed by government through legislation and legal duties.
- In any one collaboration, there is **often evidence of managers supporting different collaborative discourses,** making the search for common purpose problematic. This requires considerable negotiation and appreciation of different perspectives and understandings. There is a keen debate about how open managers need to be in the process – too much transparency risks paralysis, whereas a lack of candour poses the threat of implementation difficulties further down the policy pipeline.
- **Visions, missions, value and core purpose statements** are typical mechanisms used to formalise common purpose, but they can be woolly, ineffectual and capable of multiple interpretations. A vision or mission statement can represent a catalyst for collective action but their effectiveness needs to be tested against a number of criteria – credibility, ownership, achievability and uniqueness.
- **Understanding the perspectives of other partners** is key to collaborative negotiations – the processes involved are

'framing' where actors make sense of the realities of the world of collaboration. Frames are a reflection of an individual actors' background – social, professional and organisational; they are influenced by values and attitudes, and they function as a means of understanding the nature of public problems, their causes and potential solutions. Middle managers engaged in collaborative action bring with them a diversity of frames, which can result in conflict and dilemmas.

• **Frame articulation and understanding** is highly problematical and some middle managers have the ability to function as managers of meaning or 'frame articulators' to help others with their individual interpretations and the implications of these during the processes of negotiating common purpose.

Suggested further reading

Benford, R.D. and Snow, D.A. (2000) 'Framing processes and social movements: An overview and assessment', *Annual Review of Sociology*, Vol. 26, pp. 611–639

GAO (United States Government Accountability Office) (2005) *Results-Orientated Government: Practices that Can Help Enhance and Sustain Collaboration Among Federal Agencies*, Washington, DC: GAO

4

Managing complexity and interdependency

Everything is connected – a global economy of haves and have-nots; rising regional, international, and transnational tensions; the explosion (pun intended) of two-edged technologies that can help us or hurt us, often at the same time; climate change and all of its adverse effects; inexorable demographic trends across the globe; the list goes on. (National Academy of Public Administration, 2007: 235)

Unquestionably, the crux of a middle manager's ability to engage effectively in collaboration is underpinned by an understanding of connections and the complexities and interdependencies that flow from them. This concerns knowledge of flows, relationships and linkages of various types over time and space – problems, organisational responsibilities, financial frameworks, governance and accountability systems and policies. The knowledge base centres on the system and how it is connected and works, and not so much on the individual constituent elements. Each middle manager participating in a collaborative is likely to provide some expertise/knowledge, but in addition, this needs to be accompanied by an understanding of how the collaborative system is structured and operates. The concept of 'wicked issues' provides one of the best explanations and justifications for collaboration – issues and problems that are cross boundary in character, socially constructed and not amenable to single organisations acting autonomously. Whether the problem is one of lack of educational attainment, poverty, crime and antisocial behaviour or sustainable development and cybercrime, the challenge for middle managers is to understand how elements are connected, and what these mean for potential collaborative engagements. Practitioners of collaboration often refer to 'seeing the bigger picture' or 'understanding the jigsaw' and how it fits together with a knowledge base of the connections and relationships – the public policy context, the organisations that are involved in delivering services around a particular wicked issue; the political and governance landscape; and funding possibilities. This narrative emphasises the 'policy aspects' of wicked issues but, as McConnell (2018) argues, it is also important to explore this notion through the lens of a 'political approach' that focuses on issues of reputation, political capital, the politics of managing dense and conflicting policy agendas and the promotion of ideological visions.

A middle manager in the Fire and Rescue Service in South Wales provides two practical examples from his policy area that demonstrate how he is able to make connections that benefit both his service and the services of his partners working together in a Community Safety Partnership.

Box 4.1: Making the connections: youth engagement programme

The case for adopting a collaborative approach to a complex and inter-connected problem was made by a middle manager of a Community Safety Partnership for a Fire and Rescue Service in Wales. He argued that too often public bodies respond independently to symptoms, not causes of problems and issues. He made the case for a collective approach to a youth engagement programme based on the following real scenario:

• A young man is at a bus stop – he is wearing a 'hoodie', jogging bottoms and trainers and smoking a 'spliff' with mates; he fits the profile of someone who is likely to set fire to a wheelie-bin, to throw stones at a fire engine, to set an alarm off by throwing a stone through a shop window, or to commit minor criminal damage to street furniture and public landscaping.

- Each one of these actions leads to a fragmented approach by a public body – the fire service if it involves arson, police if it involves criminal damage and antisocial behaviour and so on – it also affects the health service if actions involve personal harm or lifestyle, the probation service if he is on their books and any interested third sector organisations.
- The point is that there are so many different public agencies that have an interest in this 'individual', and this demands a collaborative response.

Source: Williams, 2014

Box 4.2: Making the connections: house fire safety checks

The same middle manager of a Community Safety Partnership for a Fire and Rescue Service in Wales referred to above, furnished another example to illustrate his understanding of making relationships and connections:

- The case for promoting House Fire Safety Checks is based on the scenario of Mr Jones, a vulnerable older person, accidentally setting his kitchen on fire because of a chip fat fryer. The fire service had to be mobilised to put the fire out; the health service was involved to take Mr Jones to A&E and subsequently to admit him as an inpatient for a couple of weeks; the local authority was involved because his house (rented from the local council) had to be boarded up because it did not immediately have the funds for repair; when Mr Jones was released from hospital he had to be re-housed and receive regular social care at home; his previous house deteriorated and became a honey-pot for curious youngsters, some using it as a base for antisocial behaviours which involved the police.
- A simple and low-cost House Safety Check would have advocated the use of a deep fat fryer instead of a chip fat fryer which would have prevented all the above costs.

Source: Williams, 2014

Both cases reveal considerable analytic ability and knowledge of organisational connectivity on behalf of this particular middle manager, and illustrate how the efficiency and effectiveness of public services might be improved by a focus on the shared recipients of their services. The acid question is how and whether they can re-align or re-structure their services to take these connections into account. In the case of these particular examples, the route was through individual joint projects rather than system-wide changes.

One fundamental problem of a failure to make an effective connection is manifested in the process of attempting the delivery of policy aims and expectations. Policy implementation or policy execution is an issue that bedevils the policy process in general, and it is certainly one that is highly problematical in collaborative environments. Ansell and Torfing (2017) reflect on different claims that are made to explain the problems associated with policy implementation, together with their possible solutions – such as the need for the joint consideration of both policy design and policy implementation; the inhibiting principal–agent logic implicit in New Public Management that reinforces the separation between design and execution; the potential that collaboration and deliberation between upstream and downstream actors have on blurring these boundaries; and the view that policy design should be seen as an ongoing process of innovation and adaption. These authors advance an approach referred to as 'collaborative policymaking and adaptive policy implementation' to resolve the implementation problem – collaborative policy design needing to be designed to connect actors both vertically and horizontally to improve the knowledge base, enhance innovation and build joint ownership, and to be conceived as an 'ongoing process that flexibly adapts as implementation unfolds' (Ansell and Torfing, 2017: 477). They argue that a move needs to be made from programmed implementation to adaptive implementation to respond to dynamic situations characterised by uncertainty and conflict, and that 'we should not aim to "roll out" new policies like a blanket, but rather "rub them in" by feeling your way through the specific context and contingencies of implementation' (Ansell and Torfing, 2017: 477). This problem of the separation between design and implementation previously discussed is a considerable one for middle managers. The tendency is for this group of managers to be involved in the implementation rather than design stages particularly in the context of deliberately planned strategies. This can be problematical as middle managers play an important role in delivery and if they are not fully committed to the strategy, they can resist and subvert the strategic aspirations of top management in many different ways, both in terms of their own behaviours and more particularly in relation to the staff and teams they manage. Such actions attract accusations of being saboteurs of change, criticisms that might well be avoided if they were considered more as a strategic asset with an important role to play in the design of strategy and policy as well as its implementation (Currie and Procter, 2005; Floyd and Wooldridge, 1997).

The importance of responding to the issues of complexity in a rapidly changing policy environment has led to a National Academy of Public Administration report (2007: 114) calling for the development and deployment of new competencies and capabilities in managers and leaders to address them. The report argues that two new concepts need to be embraced as follows:

1. the need to confront complexity as both a risk aggravator and an opportunity;
2. to recognise that any significant government performance or outcome is necessarily co-produced by multiple actors from inside and outside government.

Leaders – whether political or career – who will be effective in deploying these concepts must be capable of challenging existing assumptions regarding organisational structure, governing frameworks and presumed constraints associated with titles, roles and position descriptions that inhibit innovation. 'They must lead across boundaries. They must reject the notion that inevitable "wicked problems" and "black swans" are too hard to tackle. They must accept the challenge to create the art of the possible where none appears to exist'. The report (2007: 115) goes on to state that:

complexity becomes a risk aggravator when its effects cannot be managed within existing policies, procedures, doctrine, legal authorities, or contractual relationships. This in turn becomes a leadership challenge because multiple entities must generally co-produce the needed outcomes. We will not see a complex problem in our lifetime where the needed outcome will not be co-produced.

A point worthy of recognition is that, from the study of complexity science, complexity does not mean consisting of a large number of parts and pieces, which is perhaps a common understanding of many managers – in other words, being complicated. Rather, complexity is grounded in an interconnectedness and dynamic interaction between different parts that cannot be predicted – and that: 'this complexity results in novel features (e.g. self-organisation) usually referred to as emergent properties' (Uhl-Bien and Marion, 2009: 642). A prime example of this concerns the issue of 'unplanned care' in the Welsh NHS outlined in Box. 4.3.

Box 4.3: The complexity of unscheduled care services

A perennial but increasingly intransigent example of a complex issue is 'unscheduled care' – felt most acutely by the NHS, but with significant ramifications and implications for a wide variety of other agencies. Unscheduled care embraces a myriad of health problems both in terms of scale and nature stemming from major incidents to people presenting themselves at Accident and Emergency services. By their very nature, they are difficult to plan for, but their implications can impact considerably on planned and elective surgery and other interventions. Unscheduled care is partly determined by the availability of different referral routes – GP practices and out-of-hours services, local pharmacies, self-management and physical proximity to Accident and Emergency services; they relate to the capacity and capability of primary care services, and the relationship between these and secondary care services. There is no standardisation and it can be described as somewhat of a 'postcode lottery'. Apart from Local Health Boards, this problem has implications for a variety of other agencies – the Ambulance Trust, GP practitioners, the police, care and nursing homes, local government especially social services and children's services, and third sector partners.

It is a complex issue because of the nature of the problem, the number of actors and organisations involved, and the continuum of possible solutions. The diversity of actors and agencies is complicated because of their individual funding mechanisms, systems of accountability, performance management regimes, decision-making processes and professional allegiances. Local government has been particularly badly affected by severe austerity measures affecting their capacity to deliver effective social care and community services. Middle managers and others, operating in this environment, do so largely in a fragmented and disjointed manner.

Efforts to plan for 'unscheduled care' through annual NHS Winter Plans (prepared in collaboration with partners) have generally failed to cope with subsequent pressures, leading to a suspension of, or delays in elective work for cancers and other life-threatening conditions with consequences felt for a number of months. Arguably, the problem is only ameliorated, not resolved. A paradigm shift is needed in terms of solutions, such as a fundamental integration of health and social care, and recognition that considerable pressures are a result of an elderly population who are prone to ill-health. Community resilience solutions that address the causes of ill-health in older people – keeping people warm, preventing them from falling and ensuring that they eat and drink properly – would be effective. Such a strategy would require a multi-agency approach, involving timescales that are both immediate and inter-generational. An added level of complexity to this issue concerns its relationship to another complex issue – 'bed blocking'. A number of older people are occupying expensive beds in hospitals because of the dearth of rehabilitation and community-based support services run by local authorities and partners.

The issues involved in this example resonate with the behaviours of a complex system (Holland, 2014) – the interactions involved are non-linear in character, rather there is evidence of emergent behaviour; chaotic behaviour where small changes can produce large changes and unbalance the whole system; and adaptive interactions where the interacting agents modify their strategies as they accumulate experience.

Another example of a complex adaptive system is the system of social interactions associated with renewal in large, complex organisations such as public bureaucracies (Floyd and Wooldridge, 2000: 41). Typically, here,

> control is highly dispersed, with many agents acting in parallel; there are multiple levels of organisation, with agents at one level serving as building blocks for agents at a higher level but with structural relationships subject to constant revision and rearrangement; and a host of imperfectly smart agents behaving in ways consistent with their intentions and expectations about the future.

The central thrust of this chapter is that one of the essential requirements of an effective collaborative middle manager is an ability to understand the complex framework and scaffolding underpinning collaborative purpose. The knowledge base for this does not depend so much on bodies of discrete information that typifies professional areas of study and expertise, but on the connections, relationships and linkages between them – the organisations that make up the governance framework, the services they discharge and the relationships of their services to their users and communities. It is predicated on understanding how the complexity of contemporary problems and issues become entangled, and embroiling many organisations in their web of responsibilities. Understanding the context for collaboration is critical – statutory responsibilities, financial frameworks and political priorities which make up the pieces of the 'jigsaw'. In the view of one middle manager: "This requires good analytical skills – to look at all different angles – and understand complexity and being an expert on connections and relationships – how the jigsaw fits together – and understanding the political landscape and associated governance issues." How this collaborative knowledge base is or can be acquired is an interesting question. Does it come through experience? Is it a consequence of working in other organisations to acquire an inter-organisational and intersectoral knowledge base? Is it through some form of education, training and development or a mix of all?

Learning and knowledge management

Appreciating and managing the complex and entangled web of interdependencies and relationships in a collaborative arena is hugely dependent upon the prevailing learning and knowledge management (KM) structures, processes and mechanisms. In turn, these are pivotal in the search for creativity, innovation and entrepreneurship that are so important in the realisation of collaborative potential between people and organisations. The literature on learning and KM is voluminous, with inter-disciplinary and contested literatures, often treated as two separate bodies, and with an over-reliance on the private sector as the main source of theorising and empirical research (LaPalombara, 2003; Rashman et al, 2009). However, a number of researchers (Inkpen, 2000; Hannah and Lester, 2009) consider that these should be integrated because of the close relationship between the two phenomena (Vera and Crossan, 2005). Both are complex and attract varying interpretations. Learning is conceptualised in different dimensions: levels (Crossan et al, 1999; Child et al, 2005); modes (Pawlowsky et al, 2001); types, for instance, single and double loop (Argyris and Schon, 1996), operational and conceptual (Lane, 2003) and exploratory and exploitative (Jansen et al, 2009); and stages or phases (Kolb, 1984). The determinants of learning (Child, 2003) include partner intentions and learning capacity that, in turn, are conditional on the transferability of knowledge, receptivity (time, resources, attitudes), competence (absorptive capacity and skills) and previous experience. Knowledge is typically divided into two types – explicit knowledge that is easily codified and communicated, and tacit knowledge which is not easy to capture, translate or transfer between different cultures, professions and agencies (Schein, 2004; De Long and Fahey, 2000). These perspectives have very interesting implications for middle managers operating in theatres of collaboration including, that learning takes place at an individual level; that it can be basic in the form of single loop learning or more profound in relation to double loop learning; and that it can progress along different stages or phases. In the main, explicit knowledge should be able to be transferred between people and organisations, sometimes mediated by issues of privacy and confidentiality, but tacit knowledge – arguably the most valuable type of knowledge and guarded jealously by some professionals, is more difficult to share. What is most important for policy and practice, are the determinants of learning and KM and whether these occur spontaneously or can be the subject of planned strategies.

Theorising about learning and KM is differentiated between structural and interpretive approaches, the former emphasise interventions affecting organisational structures, communication, absorptive capacity (Cohen and Levinthal, 1990; Lane and Lubatkin, 1998), resource frameworks and strategic planning (Dalkir, 2011), while the latter focus on meaning, culture (Rai, 2011) and sense-making, with socialisation processes, particularly in the context of communities of practice (Brown and Duguid, 1991; Wenger, 1998), providing the media through which shared understandings can be exchanged and moderated. The degree of 'social distance' between groups creates the greatest difficulties for collective learning, although a fine balance may be necessary between promoting cognitive proximity to engender mutual understanding and collaboration, and cognitive distance to encourage innovation and creativity (Nooteboom, 2008). Socialisation is also seen as the focus of tacit knowledge-orientated activities, and the cultivation of trusting relationships underpins the collaborative learning process (Lane, 2003), helping to heighten awareness and transparency between organisations, communicating objectives and assessing inter-dependencies (Parise and Prusak, 2006). The accumulation of social capital, grounded in common values and norms, facilitates knowledge transfer, but is both time-consuming and costly to produce (Inkpen, 2000).

The interplay between structure and agency are captured in the contested debate as to whether learning is an individual or collective phenomenon. On the one hand, Child et al (2005: 272) argues that individuals can only create knowledge and organisations can only provide suitable frameworks and contexts for this to happen. On the other hand, although agreeing that individuals are active agents of organisational learning, Huysman (1999) argues that structural conditions, such as cultures, power relationships, norms and rules, mediate the process. Organisations that embark upon explicit and organisation-wide learning strategies are referred to as 'learning organisations' (Senge, 1990; Palmer and Hardy, 2000), although Huysman (1999) suggests that such approaches underplay the role of spontaneous, accidental and unplanned processes. The role of agency is captured in references to key actors (Salk and Simonin, 2005), referred to as knowledge champions or brokers, who have an important role to perform in learning and KM processes. Influential middle managers can certainly adopt these roles. A number of analytical frameworks offer theoretical and practical constructs for understanding the inter-relationships between structural and agential factors. For instance, Nonaka's (1994) model for tacit and explicit knowledge conversion implies that particular structures, processes and carriers facilitate different forms of knowledge conversion and management. Box 4.4. Illustrates how this framework can be used in a case study of a service for mental health users.

Box 4.4: Processes of knowledge conversion

Nonaka's (1994) model for tacit and explicit knowledge conversion provides a useful framework for interrogating such practices in collaboration. The model implies that particular structures, processes and carriers facilitate different forms of knowledge conversion and management. A case study of integration in a recovery service for mental health users identified these processes as follows:

• **Socialisation**: examples of the transfer of tacit knowledge between professional groups of managers included networking, communities of practice and multi-disciplinary team working. This reflected a preference articulated by actors for learning from colleagues within informal settings rather than through more structured and desk-based arrangements. This type of learning is predominantly operational (Lane, 2003) in nature, rooted in the day-to-day practice of service delivery, but has the potential for co-producing new knowledge through integrated practices. The potential for generic working is also conditional upon sharing tacit knowledge, although this was limited in the case study, and complicated by the tension between blurring boundaries to achieve inter-professional flexibility, and preserving absolute clarity to protect professional integrity and accountability.

- **Externalisation**: the process of capturing tacit knowledge into an explicit form through mechanisms such as best practice, workshops and presentations.
- **Combination**: the explicit to explicit conversion of knowledge reflected in information sharing protocols, unified assessment procedures and compatible IT systems.
- **Internalisation**: limited explicit to tacit conversion achieved through the accumulated evidence of progress reports to management boards supplemented by anecdotal verification.

Source: Williams, 2012b

In a similar vein, Carlile (2004) develops a model that focuses on managing knowledge across different types of boundary, where knowledge is seen as both a source of, and barrier to innovation. It is worth exploring this model in a little depth because it offers a useful tool for examining knowledge management between actors and organisations involved in collaboration, and for designing strategies for improving the effectiveness of it. Carlile notes that traditionally there are three different perspectives on boundaries – information-processing that views knowledge as a thing to store or receive; interpretive approaches that highlight the importance of common meaning in order to share knowledge between actors; and political approaches that acknowledge how different interests can impede knowledge sharing. He also suggests that knowledge has particular properties at the boundary – difference as a result of the assemble of a range of domain-specific knowledge bases; dependence – where actors appreciate the need to coordinate tasks/contributions to achieve some kind of shared purpose; and novelty in the form of new ideas, initiatives or innovations. It is not difficult to apply this to collaborative endeavours – where different actors, often professionals, come to the table with domain-specific knowledge – acquired through their professional training and organisational/sectoral experience; where dependency on each other to realise a common purpose is appreciated; and where new ideas/innovations/practices championed by particular actors are sometimes difficult to share and distribute because of their perceived implications. Carlile (2004: 557) makes the point that 'as the number of dependencies increase between actors, the complexity and amount of effort required to share and access knowledge at a boundary also increases', which might explain some of the difficulties faced by large and diverse collaborations such as Public Service Boards in Wales.

Carlile develops a framework that combines three progressively complex boundaries – syntactic, semantic and pragmatic – with three increasingly complex processes – transfer, translation and transformation. It differentiates between domain-specific knowledge and common knowledge to better understand boundary management. Briefly, the framework consists of:

• Syntactic or information processing boundaries and involves transferring knowledge – this is relatively unproblematic and mainly concerns the processing, storage and transference of knowledge. However, in practice problems associated with confidentiality, the compatibility of IT systems and data types bedevil such processes, and they are limited to the handling of explicit rather than tacit knowledge.
• Semantic or interpretive boundaries involving the translation of knowledge. The key problem with this type of boundary is that they tend to be characterised by an absence of shared meanings on key issues between actors because of the manner in which they 'frame' issues and problems discussed above. A number of strategies can be invoked to help encourage shared meanings, understandings and approaches including, co-location of agencies/functions, cross-functional teams; shared approaches and methodologies, communities of practice; and the deployment of 'boundary spanners' to work between actors. Some actors – middle managers – are useful in this process as 'frame articulators'.
• Pragmatic or political boundaries involving the transformation of knowledge – acknowledging that 'novelty' can have a differential benefit on different actors that can impede their

ability to share/access knowledge. The need, therefore, is to work towards the transformation of knowledge that invariably requires negotiation and patience. The emphasis is on the creation of common interests to share knowledge – in public service collaborations this might be achieved through a focus on shared service users and citizens. The messenger sometimes influences the receptivity by some actors to 'novelty' – whether it is being imposed by government, championed by a particular professional group, or the product of a different culture and ways of working by individuals or agencies. The use of specific 'boundary objects' to mediate these complex processes at this boundary can be considered a worthwhile investment and these are discussed overleaf.

Specifically in a public service context, Rashman et al (2009) highlight power, politics and leadership as important influencing factors within inter-organisational learning; Bate and Roberts (2002) underline social and informal aspects; Nicolini et al (2008) emphasise the benefits of networks and communities of practice in the dispersal of knowledge; and Currie and Suhomlinova (2006) highlight the cultural and political dimensions of knowledge sharing in practice. Dunlop and Radaelli (2018: 257) argue that: 'the features, triggers, hindrances and pathologies of learning depend on the policy process context in which actors interact' and that 'learning has different qualities and logics depending on this tone' set by this context – epistemic (or knowledge-driven), reflexivity, bargaining and compliance with hierarchy. Although knowledge-driven learning based on professional expertise is important in collaboration, arguably, reflective learning centred around: 'deliberations involving a wide range of social actors of myriad backgrounds who bring a range of codified and un-codified knowledge types to bear on debate' (Dunlop and Radaelli, 2018: 260) conducted within an open, deliberative and non-judgemental context, and learning as a by-product of bargaining, are more applicable to collaborative situations.

Boundary object perspectives

The use of boundary object theory to understand policy and practice in settings where multiple stakeholders with multiple interests need to be able to collaborate is as yet an underdeveloped but promising area of research. Star and Griesemer (1989: 393) describe boundary objects as:

> Those scientific objects which both inhabit several intersecting social worlds...and satisfy the informational requirements of each of them. Boundary objects are objects which are both plastic enough to adapt to local needs and the constraints of the several parties employing them, yet robust enough to maintain a common identity across sites. They are weakly structured in common use, and become strongly structured in individual-site use. These objects may be abstract or concrete. They have different meanings in different social worlds but their structure is common enough to more than one world to make them recognizable, a means of translation. The creation and management of boundary objects is a key process in developing and maintaining coherence across intersecting social worlds.

Boundary objects are represented in a variety of forms, including tangible artifacts such as reports, processes and systems, discourses, narratives, concepts, theories and dominant ideologies. Some boundary objects act as a means of translation, enabling actors from different backgrounds to collaborate without losing the particular language that is rooted into their own specific organisational, sectoral or professional constituencies. What is important is that boundary objects can help to create new identities between diverse actors serving to focus their attention on some form of common purpose – for instance, membership of a new multi-disciplinary team or inter-agency group. It is likely that collaborative boundaries will be encased in a 'boundary infrastructure' of different objects nested at different levels of governance and scale (Bowker and Star, 1999; Thomas et al, 2007). The influence of power is inescapable in boundaries and there is a keen debate as to whether boundary objects are 'anchors and bridges' or 'barricades and mazes' (Oswick and Robertson, 2009) that promote conflict by reinforcing the status quo rather than facilitating new shared understandings. Undoubtedly, boundary objects are not apolitical, but have a mediating rather than a performative role; they are capable of interpretation; riven with tension and ambiguity; and frequently the subject of constant re-evaluation and negotiation. Emphasising a point made in the previous chapter about the role of vision and mission statement, visionary boundary objects are more likely to have a general appeal because they are conceptual, whereas more precise boundary objects generate contestation (Barrett and Oborn, 2010). The value of boundary object theory lies in the relationship between objects and agency. Different actors – in the case of this book, middle managers – have an important relational and mediating influence evidenced, for instance, in Carlile's (2004) work on managing relationships and building trust across syntactic and semantic boundaries, and more generally within the context of learning and knowledge management.

Boundary object theory offers a potentially valuable tool for exploring the role and influence of boundary objects in collaborative settings, particularly those that involve the agency of middle managers. For example, Table 4.1 catalogues the range and type of boundary objects – the boundary infrastructure – that exist around the notion of a locality model for the integration of health and social care in one area of South Wales.

This infrastructure consists of a number of different types of boundary object – some physical, such as the co-location of services, and unified IT systems, but others that relate more directly to agency through management and professional practice. However, picking up a point made previously, physical objects are invariably the subject of multiple interpretations and understandings. For example, co-location is a physical object that can also function as a powerful symbolic device. The case for physically co-locating previously separate health and social care services is compelling in terms of resources, communication and management, providing the environment for integrated

Table 4.1: Boundary objects in the locality model of integration in health and social care

	Boundary object	Type
Co-location of services	Buildings	Physical artefact
Integrated leadership and management	Individual leader/manager	Agent/actor
Shared or pooled budgets	Statutory instrument	Policy tool
Common approach and assessment frameworks	Policy instrument	Professional practice
Integrated governance and accountability	Governance system	Management structure
Multi-disciplinary teams	Team	Group structure
Common performance management frameworks	Policy instrument	Professional practice
Unified IT and information sharing systems and protocols	Operational support system	Physical structure and system

activities between different actors to prosper, removing the physical barriers to personal and professional interactions, and making it easier for relationships and networks to flourish. This symbolism is as important for service users as it is for staff. However, the extent to which co-location as a boundary object performed as 'an anchor or bridge' is debatable because of the continuation of separate management, budgeting and staffing arrangements. It could be argued that it serves as a façade to shield existing professional status, power and related boundaries.

Some boundary objects are potentially transformational in that they offer particular models or approaches to public policy and practice. They act as sense making devices – critiquing existing approaches and providing the stimulus for change. For example, the notion of 'integration' offers a radical new way of designing and delivering health and social care services. However, it may contain sufficient 'plasticity' to be understood by different constituencies and be a 'rallying-call' to action, but in practice its operationalisation is open to wide interpretation. In the case study above, 'its role was both facilitative and inhibitory (Fox, 2011), facilitative as it helped to promote the general virtues of integration both internally and externally, and inhibitory as its interpretive flexibility allowed different actors to pursue separate paths so limiting the possibility of whole-system change' (Sullivan and Williams, 2012).

Models as boundary objects can also function as a means of understanding – imbued as they are by values and attitudes acquired through education and training, and jealously guarded by professional bodies. The multiple framing of 'health' is one such example making progress on integration in health and social care problematic – professional medical groups generally supporting a medical model and social workers the social model. This apparent polarisation can, however, be countered through sensitive and sustained negotiation between respective constituencies. For example, in the case of a mental health recovery service (Williams, 2017) a new model was developed sufficient to function as the basis for integrated and multi-disciplinary practice. It was premised on delivering a personalised service within the community with high levels of user involvement, as opposed to a previous model described as paternalistic, group-focused and delivered in a traditional residential setting. Interviewees from both health and social care backgrounds claimed the new model was able to 'transcend all boundaries' – professional, sectoral and organisational – especially as it encapsulated all that actors valued in an integrated service in terms of purpose, values and principles.

Middle managers in collaboration might usefully reflect on the contribution of Fong et al (2007: 16) in their reference to the role of a systems integrator. They take the view that: 'the value of a boundary object depends on how successfully it can be used to decontextualise knowledge on one side of a boundary and recontextualise it on the other side'. The systems integrator's role is to manage the boundary interfaces between different communities of practice. This role is premised on an understanding of the nature and role of particular boundary objects that they characterise on their type, functionality, utility, granularity, context and familiarity between the user groups. An analysis of the potential of a particular boundary object will assist a middle manager in its selection, deployment and management.

Table 4.2: Characteristics of a boundary object

Characteristic	Description
Type	Virtual and physical. Virtual boundary objects are those that exist in bytes and bits, e.g. emails, websites and electronic databases. Physical boundary objects are objects that are tangible and can be physically manipulated.
Functionality	Four functional categories: • Repositories are ordered collections of objects such as a library or database. • Ideal types are abstractions from different domains and may be open to a fairly broad spectrum of interpretation. • Coincident boundaries are common objects which have the same boundaries but different internal contents, e.g. co-located offices. • Standardised forms are objects that provide different communities with a common way to communicate.
Utility	The utility is the degree of cognitive usefulness the user finds in the object, measuring the degree in which the object will influence the user's task.
Granularity	Granularity describes the level of detail (the amount and type) of the information in the boundary object.
Context	The context of the boundary object describes how well it addresses the different social contexts and mental models of the user groups. These differences can lead to understanding gaps and some communities may be able to understand each other better than others through their mental model alignment.
Familiarity	Familiarity of the stakeholder's involved – e.g. previous partnerships and contractual agreements – can promote the acceptance of boundary objects, particularly as a result of increased trust.
Synchronisation	A change in the information in one object must propagate to other tightly coupled objects requiring appropriate configuration management processes.

Source: Adapted from Fong et al, 2007

The middle manager as systems integrator in Fong et al's (2007: 17) visualisation needs to appreciate that: 'certain types of boundary objects will be more effective in some environments as compared to others. Boundary objects can be used to measure the fluidity and flexibility of different constituent systems', and that they need to cultivate an environment that encourages the effectiveness of different objects in pursuit of collaborative advantage for all parties.

Key points of learning

- **Understanding complexity, relationships and interdependencies** is an integral component of a middle manager's ability to engage effectively in collaboration.
- It is this capability that constitutes the core of **'collaborative knowledge'** that is essential for operating in collaboration and making sense of the 'collaborative jigsaw' puzzle.
- **Policy implementation** is a particular issue of the collaborative policy process and the absence of integration and connectedness between the various elements and actors involved.
- Appreciating and managing the complex and entangled web of interdependencies and relationships in a collaborative arena is hugely dependent upon the prevailing **learning and knowledge management (KM)** structures, processes and mechanisms. These are pivotal in the search for creativity, innovation and entrepreneurship.
- **Lessons for middle managers** operating in collaboration include, that learning takes place at an individual level; that it can be basic in the form of single loop learning or more profound in relation to double loop learning; and that it can progress along different stages or phases.
- Explicit knowledge can be transferred between people and organisations relatively straightforwardly, but tacit knowledge is often guarded jealously by some professionals, and is more difficult to share. Nonaka's (1994) **model for tacit and explicit knowledge conversion** provides a useful framework for interrogating such mechanisms in collaboration. The model implies that particular structures, processes and carriers facilitate different forms of knowledge conversion and management. Carlile's (2004) model of managing knowledge across different types of boundary – syntactic, semantic and pragmatic.

- A **key question for policy and practice**, is whether the determinants of learning and KM and occur spontaneously or can be the subject of planned strategies.
- **Boundary object theory** offers a valuable tool for exploring the role and influence of boundary objects in collaborative settings, particularly those that involve the agency of middle managers.

Suggested further reading

Dierkes, M., Berthoin Antal, A., Child, J. and Nonaka, I. (2003) *Handbook of Organisational Learning and Knowledge*, Oxford: Oxford University Press

National Academy of Public Administration (2007) *Building a 21st Century SES: Ensuring Leadership Excellence in Our Federal Government*, Washington, DC: National Academy of Public Service

Nonaka, I. (1994) 'A dynamic theory of organisational knowledge creation', *Organisation Science*, Vol. 5 (1), pp. 15–37

Prusak, L. and Matson, E. (2006) *Knowledge Management and Organisational Learning: A Reader*, Oxford: Oxford University Press

5

Managing relationships

> Well, now, here's the thing about trust. There's nothing to it. Trusting people is simply a matter of ignoring your best instincts and all your experience and suspending belief. The fact is, the only way you can ever be sure if you can rely on someone or not is to go ahead and rely on them. But that doesn't always work out so well. People usually behave like people and let you down and that's that. Of course, if you know they're going to let you down then you won't be disappointed. (Kerr, 2018)

There is a keen debate as to whether particular organisational structures and frameworks enable or obstruct collaborative working, or whether outcomes are largely dependent upon agency – the commitment and behaviour of like-minded managers and other actors working together to achieve results that could not be realised by them acting independently. Certainly, a strong consensus of views from a wide range of middle managers in my research in Wales comes down on the side of agency, as is suggested by this selection of opinions:

- "You can have the best, most effective and streamlined structures, but if people can't trust each other, any partnership will fail."
- "The thing that makes it work in any type of structure is the commitment of the person – structures can be enabling or difficult."

- "It isn't about organisations getting on with one another, it's individuals sitting around a table. It's about trust between individuals – me knowing who to contact, who is going to be an ally and who I need to work on; each individual has his/her reputation; I'm someone who says it, and does it; I am straight to the point and tell it as it is; people need to be prepared to put the energy into personal relationships – it's about finding people who want to talk and nurturing that relationship; that's the way to influence people."
- "Honesty is what sees relationships through tough times" and "I have to look my colleagues in the eye knowing I haven't pulled the rug from under their feet."

In a study of a cadre of middle managers in a Welsh local council, the essence of working effectively in collaboration was widely considered to be dependent upon building and sustaining relationships with all the stakeholders involved. There were frequent references to 'trust' as the glue or mechanism that facilitated these exchange relationships, and to 'networking' as the process by which these relationships were cultivated and maintained. Building social capital through networking was seen by one middle manager as: "a natural extension of the challenges involved in working inter-departmentally – and the need to build a network of friends over the years".

There are a number of points of interest that can be inferred from this statement. First, this middle manager is making comparisons between inter-departmental work and working in collaboration with people in outside agencies. In some highly functionally- or professionally-organised agencies, boundary challenges can be appreciable, and experience of managing these through cross-departmental and other mechanisms are a useful education for collaboration across organisational and sectoral boundaries. Working across the internal boundaries of an organisation might be framed by a unified corporate structure and system of accountability, but power, politics, culture, profession, status, legal and statutory duties and performance imperatives, play an important part in working towards corporate objectives and purpose. The focus on managing personal and professional relationships is paramount in these encounters.

Second, the importance of devoting time to relationship building was stressed, with consistency and regular communication between contacts. The opportunity of working with middle managers in other organisations over a sustained period of time – meeting on a face to face basis either individually or at meetings, telephone conversations, and email exchanges – was seen as the best way of building personal and professional relationships. It helps build trust, understanding and empathy – some of the precursors for an effective relationship. A network of relationships between middle managers in a particular geographical or policy area can also be extremely valuable in sustaining and developing new forms of collaboration based on previous experience and contacts.

Last, the reference to the cultivation of personal (friends) as well as professional contacts is important. This point was underscored by a frequently voiced irritant of a number of middle managers who bemoaned some organisations sending inappropriate people to represent them on collaborations. One middle manager stated that: "getting a person there is not enough – it has to be the right person". The 'right person' is not always easy to identify. It can be a straightforward matter of status and a view that representing an organisation can only be done by middle managers of a certain status irrespective of whether they are suited to the task; it can be a matter of motivation and whether a particular representative is perceived to be open to collaboration or merely protecting the interests of their organisation; or it can be a matter of competence and ability to work effectively in a collaborative setting. A view from one local government middle manager was that: "who you select to go on working groups need not necessarily be the most senior – you need personable and skilled people and this shouldn't be done on status – some people work well above their grade" and another manager referred to: "not having people stuck up their own backsides and being overly precious – getting the 'right 'people at the table who focus on delivery is the most important thing".

The point about the importance of time is relevant here again. It does take time to build and sustain relationships – to understand other people's motivations and ways of working;

judging whether they can be trusted; valuing their expertise and contributions; and having the satisfaction of being part of successful joint endeavour. However, given the time that collaborative working often involves, consistency of representation is not always guaranteed. People get promoted or move away – and the internal dynamics of collaborative working groups are compromised, with new personalities and new relationships having to be forged. The success of a collaborative project in South Wales (Pathways to Work Project providing a single gateway to financial, employment and health support for people claiming incapacity benefits) was partly attributed to middle managers from different agencies having worked with each other over a period of time on a number of different initiatives. An unpublished evaluation report concluded that interviewees were of the view that:

> Considerable social capital had accumulated between a network of key players enabling joint action to be undertaken in a climate of an understanding of respective individual and organisational roles, responsibilities and ways of working. Key individuals associated with the Condition Management Programme considered themselves to be part of what one respondent referred to as 'the local partnership mafia'.

The importance of personal relationships was considered to be critical for this group with middle managers expressing confidence in their colleagues and emphasising the importance of trusting relationships and the ability to work effectively together. Typical comments included:

> "It's a very effective and well-functioning group; the people are supportive, fully engaged and see the benefits of the service; nobody seems to be professionally precious and everyone has something to contribute."

> "Discussions have been open and frank from the start."

The reference to not being 'professionally precious' is a salutary lesson for middle managers working in collaboration. The clear message is that core professional bodies of expertise and knowledge are valued, but they must be open to scrutiny, challenge and adaptation in the light of alternative framing by middle managers with different professional backgrounds and experiences. This is not an easy task for hard-nosed middle managers whose upbringings have been encased in a particular professional bubble, and who often continue to spend a great deal of their working lives in this environment within their home organisations and overseeing professional bodies. Middle managers who are perceived by members of their own professional group or organisation to sympathise with other agencies can be accused of 'going native', making their work in collaboration difficult, and their job of persuading their own organisations to do things differently that much more challenging. It is very important for middle managers engaged in collaboration with other agencies to devise effective means of communication with their home organisation to counter these problems. Collaboration has to be seen as a legitimate form of activity to achieve an organisation's aims – not bolted-on or imposed from outside. In particular, where collaboration involves systemic changes that require 'mainstreaming' into an organisation, sustained efforts need to be put in place in order to achieve success including, clarifying rationales, outlining the benefits, detailing the implications for ways of working, and drawing up the necessary training and capacity building programmes to support the changes. The middle manager who is traditionally seen as a conduit between top management and the frontline in traditional organisations now has a pivotal role to play as a conduit between the home organisation and the collaborative. The middle manager has to devise effective methods of communication within the home organisation – ideally promoting a two-way dialogue that involves developing mechanisms to engage with a wide set of stakeholders in the home organisation, and certainly not acting independently. Of course, some middle managers might consider such a position to be valuable in terms of their personal career progression, particularly with partner organisations, and be somewhat more reticent in involving others. This is an important point to recognise because there is little doubt that an effective collaborating middle manager can bring many benefits to an organisation in terms of profile, resources and local leverage. This potential constitutes a considerable source of power for the middle manager concerned, and organisations need to recognise this, particularly in relation to reward and performance management frameworks.

The importance of an organisation to fully recognise the significance of collaboration for its ability to adapt in a rapidly changing environment is underscored by Allred et al (2011) in a private sector context in their discussion of collaboration as a 'dynamic capability' of a firm. Their research suggests that firms have a high collaborative capability if they invest in improved information sharing; promote boundary spanning initiatives; foster collaborative people skills; and align goals and metrics to develop collaboration. This involves firms changing structures and mind-sets accordingly, including, assembling people around joint problem solving and innovation, engaging in collaborative projects and developing adaptive skills in managers. The main point here is that organisations need to take steps internally to gear themselves to working in collaboration, and it should not just rely on the individual motivations and behaviours of a selected number of middle managers.

The notion of trust was foremost in the comments of middle managers interviewed in the research evaluation referred to overleaf. Many claimed that the steering group on which they were represented: "is one where you can trust your partners and there are no hidden agendas – trust is where you know that someone is not going to do the dirty on you and set you up for a fall – in this group I'm not afraid to say anything because I know I'm among friends – the catalyst for conflict in partnerships are people's personal egos – but this doesn't happen here". One of the key advantages of working in an open and trusting forum, in the view of one middle manager, was that: "I'm not afraid to challenge – I find it very frustrating when I see other agencies being nice to each other around tables, especially when you know there are real issues – people play this game around partnership tables then have different discussions outside the room." The point here is that middle managers judge that they are relatively free to disagree and argue with colleagues without fear of severing their long-term relationships. Inevitably, there may be temporary fall-outs and disagreements, but the strength of the relationship is such that it is capable of repair and ongoing collaboration. Returning to an issue mentioned earlier, this reinforces the importance of having the 'right' managers around the partnership table – those who have the competencies and mindset to work together on common aims, and not those who are merely organisational representatives dispatched to monitor any potential negative impact on their employing agency. A key question for policy and practice is whether this alchemy is a matter of luck, or whether it can be manufactured through careful selection, training and development. Certainly, it can just happen that a particular partnership group is able to gel and work together effectively – it may be because of the composition and competencies of the group, the style of leadership or many other factors. It is often reported that when a particularly key member of a group leaves for some reason, and is replaced by another, the dynamics of that group are altered and its effectiveness is compromised. It is often not possible to dictate to organisations who they send to represent them, although private feedback about an individual's performance is certainly possible. The important point though is that effective collaboration is very much determined and influenced by the ability of middle managers to work effectively both as individuals and in teams within the context of a framework of collaborative governance. It is far from a radical proposition, therefore, to suggest that such actors need the skills, competencies and experience to operate in this environment.

The importance of relationships to effective collaboration was underscored by the middle managers interviewed in a research study of a local council. A selection of opinions on relationship building and networking included the following:

- "Building relationships through informal networks – knowing who to contact – being an informational intermediary."

- "Knowing who/where to go, who is best connected and where to get resources."
- "Building social capital with 'like-minded people' who are all committed and want the same thing – I can be closer to health colleagues on a daily basis than some of my own colleagues in the council."
- "Being a social butterfly – being personable, developing relationships and networking."
- "Building up networks to access good practice – gaining support from different people in different areas – personal support, shared learning and the benefits of long-term trusting relationships."
- "The skills necessary are less about technical knowledge than my ability to know folk and for them to know me – you need to build relationships and networks."

There are a number of interesting points that emerge from these views and opinions. First, relationship building is considered to be instrumental in being able to make sense of the connectivity of policy areas and collaborative opportunities. This underscores the discussion in the previous chapter on the need to understand the interdependencies between different organisations. Contacts with middle managers in partner agencies are a considerable help in facilitating this understanding including, helping to forge a common purpose and linking up the respective contributions of, and having an impact on, different agencies. This is achieved through regular personal contacts, in and around formal meetings, and particularly at joint training and development events. The value of being able to design and deliver management-training programmes that can be made accessible to middle managers in a number of organisations can be catalytic. It helps to develop personal networks and facilitates joint learning around common agendas. Second, networking facilitates joint learning and knowledge management with colleagues from other organisations that can be used to shape the ongoing collaborative process, but also be transferred and used for the benefit of their own organisations. This was exemplified by one middle manager who highlighted the importance of networks in developing creative solutions. He remarked that:

> "When the regional collaborative fund was announced, the chief executive asked me to do something – I rang up a couple of colleagues in two other areas that I worked with 2 years ago and said – 'you've got similar NEETs (Not in Education, Employment or Training) problems to us – do you fancy collaborating – are you up for this?' – it was in place in 2 days – if I'd done it cold it would have taken ages." (Williams, 2013b)

Third, there is often an acceptance that it is perfectly possible 'to be as close' to colleagues in other organisations as it is to those in their own home organisations. Arguably, such relationships can be construed as more genuine because they are free from the constraints of power and status that exist with colleagues employed in the same organisation. Organisations can be somewhat claustrophobic in the sense that rules, roles, lines of accountability and reporting are prescribed and set a particular way of doing things – the culture. Collaboration can be potentially less structured and cathartic, with middle managers engaging with others to release the potential of cooperative actions. Last, the metaphor of being a 'social butterfly' conjures up the image of middle managers having to display extrovert personalities – to be sociable, engaging, confident, self-assured and comfortable around people from different backgrounds. This certainly may be an appropriate style for some, and there are many examples of such middle managers, but for others, the sincerity of their inter-personal relationships can be legitimately demonstrated through less flamboyant behaviours and actions. Perversely, there can be some dangers with overly extrovert behaviours, particularly when they might be used as a façade concealing more self-interested motivations.

A police superintendent in the same research study explained his view of the centrality of relationships and networking in the following terms:

"Knowing where to go and who to speak to is important, as is forging relationships over a number of years. This needs to be based on trust – bending a bit and asking for help – being able to compromise and negotiate. I am dependable and have grown up conversations with people. I can't force people to do things in collaboration, but I know they will and vice versa; although there are clear organisational borders, we are all looking to do the same thing. We need to forget about boundaries – I consider that the people I work with from other organisations are as much my colleagues as those in my own organisation."

A similar flavour to the criticality of relationship building was inherent in the following local government middle manager's reflections (Williams, 2013b):

- "You can have all the joint protocols you like but at the end of the day it comes down to personal relationships."
- "Building relationships by demonstrating integrity and a willingness to explore honestly and openly."
- "It's about people skills and building trust."
- "Open, honest and transparent – no hidden agendas –sharing difficulties – there is nothing worse than 'conversations in cupboards'."
- "Can only do business if we are honest with each other and trust each other – importance of clarity of purpose, openness, honesty and not trying to shaft them – not trying to get one over them."
- "Depends on people – if you have high levels of trust you can shift a lot of things."
- "Have to put yourself in a position to speak freely – can't be guarded – would never get proper open discussion otherwise."

These observations reflect a focus on the importance of adhering to, and practising a set of moral standards such as integrity, honesty, openness, being respectful and above all, trustworthiness.

Trust in collaborative relationships

Trust is generally considered to be at the very core of personal relationships, and its importance in collaborative settings cannot be underestimated because of the increased focus of public management on tackling complex public policy problems and issues that cross the boundaries of single organisations, and that require cooperation and collaboration between diverse actors and agencies to resolve them. 6 et al (2006: 117) suggest that:

> it is important for managers in organisations to take some pains to develop rich appreciations of the specific contextual and institutional characteristics of the network environment – and the trust relations of this environment – and to make their decisions about the strategies for trust and trustworthiness in the light of this appreciation.

Agranoff (2003: 22) comments that:

> Social capital, or the built-up reservoir of good will that flows from different organisations working together for mutual productive gain, no doubt is the 'glue' that holds people together or the 'motivator' that moves the process along. But in terms of what helps to steer networks, it is clearly trust, the obligation to be concerned with others' interests, that allows for the network to do its work, select its leaders, keep its members, and most important, to broker those decisions it must make.

Milward and Proven (2006: 10) argue that: 'the currency of a network is the trust and reciprocity that exist among its members' and 'the more trust and reciprocity in the network, the greater the ability of the network to accomplish shared goals'. They proceed to argue that: 'The task of network managers is to increase the stock of trust and reciprocity by creating incentives (using resources) and to increase their collaborative skills to build relationships within the network to accomplish network goals.' Trust involves the suspension of risk leading to cooperation, flexibility, innovation, learning and an increase in cost-effectiveness; whereas distrust encompasses regulation, behavioural control, high transaction costs and low, predicable gains. La Porte (1996: 69) conceptualises trust in public organisation networks from the vantage points of three types of networker and argues that:

> net riders seek to arrange relationships with other net members so that they can trust them and work out the efficient monitoring means to be assured that other exchange partners can continue to be trusted within a more or less fixed system of incentives. (In a sense, they seek to reduce the transaction costs of incipient suspicion.) Net throwers examine the political, legal, and economic conditions that foster or diminish the likelihood that net members will become and will stay trustworthy. Attentive outsiders seek insights about the leverage outsiders can play as monitors or enhancers of trustworthiness, or as destroyers of trusted relations.

The notion of trust has attracted a large body of inter-disciplinary literature, and consequently its understanding is fraught with ambiguity, lack of specificity and debate. Oomsels and Bouckaert's (2014) review of the dimensions of trust conclude that it is variously interpreted as an expectation, an attitude, or a behaviour. They also consider that it is individuals – boundary spanners – who are mandated by organisations to manage the interactions between organisations; and these individuals have a dual personality – a private one, and an organisational one determined by specific organisational demands. They conclude therefore that: 'in complex interorganisational interactions, the individual subjective evaluations of the boundary spanners build on their personal and organisational considerations and are therefore the basis of interorganisational trust' (Oomsels and

Bouckaert, 2014: 590). These authors proceed to develop a framework for examining trust that involves: 'a discussion of sources on the three levels of interorganisational interactions that influence subjective evaluations by boundary spanners'. These three levels are:

- Macro-level: this revolves around institution-based trust grounded in the rules, routines and role definitions that frame the working lives of boundary spanners – having both a direct influence but also an indirect one through socialisation. This sets the culture of an organisation and defines the nature of the 'bridges' – either facilitative or inhibitive – with other organisations;
- Meso-level: focuses on calculative and relational sources of trust based on familiarity, information, characteristics and dynamics;
- Micro-level: relates to individual's trusting or distrusting predispositions or tendencies irrespective of situations and connect to personality traits.

The authors argue that boundary spanners make subjective evaluations of trust and distrust on the basis of the: 'characteristics of rules, roles, routines, and dominant normative frameworks on the macro-level, by interaction-specific calculative and relational characteristics on the meso-level, and by individual predispositions on the micro-level of interorganisational interactions' (Oomsels and Bouckaert, 2014: 596). Turning to a selection of views expressed by middle managers in my research on trust outlined below, there are a number of points of confirmation with this and other literature on the subject.

"I trust no-one; trust until proven otherwise; assume people are always honest – reciprocal small steps."

"Being true to their word – honesty – gut feeling – faith – trusting person – build a relationship but continually checking it – live and learn – if it doesn't work – revisit relationship constantly in your mind – if you don't trust them you start resorting to emails and evidence trail' – low trust involves more formalised procedures and paperchecks."

"Believing what somebody tells me – committed to what they say – start with some scepticism but it grows – trust is earned – same as in social situations – taking 'baby steps' reciprocal behaviour – is he doing what he says what he'll do."

"You need some sociability to enhance trust."

"I spend 5–10 minutes before every meeting talking to people about their kids, hairdressers, holidays and what's the gossip in each organisation – its intimate personal stuff where you expose yourself to risk – that is, trust that people don't take advantage of you – you have to tell people a lot of stuff about yourself; it's doing favours – honesty and trust are the glue that bind people together."

Lane (1998) refers to common components of trust, particularly as a means of dealing with risk and uncertainty, and a hope that the other party will not abuse the vulnerability resulting from the acceptance of risk. Lane (1998) further suggests that trust can derive from a number of sources:

- Calculative – where the focus is very much on evaluation and testing out trust in practice; the 'earned' trust or 'reciprocal behaviours' and 'small steps' referred to in one of the understandings reported above. This interpretation underpins the view that trust is a dynamic and cyclical process – spiralling upward through positive experiences into 'deeper' forms of trust, but capable of descending uncontrollably if negative experiences are encountered. When the latter occurs, the problem is whether it is possible to rebuild a trusting relationship with a partner. This might be possible, but the criteria for 'trusting' are likely to be far more rigorous, and the time taken to reach previous levels of trust greater in length. The nuclear option of severing relationships completely is often not available because middle managers from one organisation cannot choose whom they work with in other organisations.

• Value or norm-based – which stems from an individual's belief that people are honest and generally act in good faith without wanting to harm others. Some middle managers report that this is their default starting position, while others take a contrary view and start with mistrusting people until their experiences prove otherwise.

• Common cognition – which refers to systems of shared meaning that Sydow (1998) considers is manifested in three types – process-based which is rooted in personal relationships including technical knowledge and expertise; characteristic-based that relates to personal characteristics and qualities; and finally, institution-based that emanates from traditions or professions. The relationship between trust and professionalism is an interesting one. The notion of professionalism is grounded on a set of individuals who, through training and experience, and supported, accredited and regulated by their professional bodies, can be 'trusted' by the public to act to the highest standards and in good faith. This may indeed be the case but an alternative narrative suggests that some professions can be narrow-minded and act only in the interests of their members and their particular professional values. These can be at odds with one another when different professional groups are required to work together in collaboration. For instance, in the challenge of integration of health and social care systems, health professionals often express a fundamentally different view of 'health' to their social care partners. The former seeing it as essentially a matter of 'illness and sickness' while the latter viewing it much more broadly in the context of the determinants of health. The notion of sustainable development equally attracts fundamentally divergent interpretations, with environmentalists clinging to the view that it is essentially a question of preserving the natural environment, as opposed to those who take a much broader view suggesting that it is more a balance between economic development, social equality, and environmental protection in the context of both current and future generations.

Agranoff (2003) found that: 'the process of mutual learning through exploration leads to additional trust', that 'procedurally the consensus-building process builds trust', and that 'trust is maintained by non-encroachment on any participating agency's domain'. Trust is often considered to lie in the relationships between people at a personal and individual level, but there is a view that it can be manifested at a macro level discussed overleaf. Certain organisations gain a reputation, rightly or wrongly, for being good to work with, whereas others attract the reverse standing. This could be a reflection of a particular organisational culture or the product of the accumulated behaviours of actors within them over a period of time. There are often references to 'a history of partnership' existing in a particular geographical area or between a number of agencies, where levels of trust are considered to be healthy. In these situations, particularly where there have been previous experiences of effective collaboration and positive outcomes, the situation is ripe for further collaboration when opportunities arise, or problems are encountered. It is much easier to re-instate a previous collaborative machinery against a backdrop of high social capital and trusting relationships between actors, than to have to start a process from the beginning. If a body of key middle managers endure, the collaborative process can have a 'kick start', particularly as Agranoff (2003: 23) observes: 'trust can also be built through progressive accomplishment'. Conversely of course, where the history of partnership working in an area has not been positive, engaging in collaboration can be problematic from the outset.

Although it is right to consider that trust is the medium of exchange – the glue and the lubricant – that facilitates the course of collaboration, some commentators suggest that it can be commandeered by some middle managers as an alternative source of power – when other sources more familiar to them operating within organisations – are not available. Hardy et al (1998) refers to this as a façade of trust where managers use it to manipulate others. Naturally, this may be difficult to detect in practice but inauthentic proponents of this art are arguably ultimately found out! Perhaps an overriding reflection of trust lies in its inherent fragility. Collaborations consist of a highly complicated scaffold of trusting relationships; of different types and at different levels. It is dynamic and exceedingly susceptible to external reverberations in the form of government policy, political priorities, pressure on resources, performance and scrutiny issues and customer expectations. An interesting question relates to the extent to which the strength of trusting personal relationship can act as a buffer to these external shocks, or whether their brittleness results in them being broken rendering the collaboration less effective?

The leadership role of the middle manager

Contemporary public service organisations are complex bureaucracies consisting of multiple stakeholders, interests and professional practices framed within a highly politicised environment and characterised by boundary crossing interactions both within and between agencies. The ensuing leadership challenge for such organisations is considerable, and the leadership literature and practices have more recently moved away from a preoccupation with formally appointed and top leaders (important as they still are) to a view that leadership functions and activities need to be shared, dispersed and distributed (Pearce and Conger, 2003; Gronn, 2002) among a much wider set of actors at all levels of an organisational hierarchy. Turnbull James (2011: 6) captures this view of leadership as 'postheroic' which: 'involves multiple actors who take up leadership roles both formally and informally, and importantly, share leadership by working collaboratively, often across organisational or professional boundaries' and as a consequence, 'that leadership needs to be understood in terms of leadership practices and organisational interventions rather than just personal behavioural style or competences; the focus is on organisational relations, connectedness, interventions into the organisational system, and changing organisational practices and processes'. The implications of this form of leadership for middle managers are profound both in terms of their management within and between organisations. Leadership is less hierarchical in nature – as much bottom up as top down – and focused around building relationships and networks, and: 'roles may even change, with someone labeled "leader" in one situation but "follower" with the same people in others' (Turnbull James, 2011: 5).

The potential of this type of leadership is cathartic for middle managers who aspire to, and practice, collaborative management. The presence of multiple stakeholders with varying degrees and sources of power and leverage make directive and dictatorial approaches both inappropriate and unrealistic in practice. Collaboration is a collective endeavour that requires facilitative, enabling and above all shared approaches to realise the potential of a diverse constituency. It can be argued, therefore, that leadership approaches have of necessity to be of a particular type in collaboration, as opposed to single organisations where there is a choice between different approaches. However, a middle manager from an organisation that does promote shared leadership approaches might be in a good position to continue with the same in collaborative settings. One middle manager working in an integrated care setting reflected that it was very challenging to operate in different governance arrangements:

> "It is not natural to go from one to another because it is different; it is complex; you need to think about your partner before taking action; you must give stuff up – including power to gain influence; it's about relationships and trust; it involves acting as an interpreter for your own organisation about your partners; it's about loyalty to your organisation and staying faithful to your partners; there are new leadership skills and cultures for integration."

The presumption here being that the leadership cultures in both forms of governance is different. Middle managers working in collaboration assume a range of roles in this form of governance. It typically involves representing their home organisation – both informally and formally – on various forms of working groups, task forces and committees – sometimes taking a formal leader role but at other times being a participant. One middle manager in a formal leadership role was described as being:

> "Humble but firm and directive; very nice but not weak; very respectful; listens and makes good eye contact; very knowledgeable in general but able to admit lack of knowledge where it exists; does his homework; uses humour; inspires; does not shut me out; searches you out informally to check if everything is OK; makes time for you; searches around for ideas; is grounded and never looks flustered."

In a similar vein, another middle manager suggested that leadership needed to be:

> "Sensitive to the differences of various partners; needing to talk and listen to people; to take their advice and trust others."

An interesting reflection on leadership was raised by one middle manager in relation to gender. She remarked that:

> "Leadership needs to be focussed but not alpha-male – because you can't tell people what to do – it needed the application of softer skills – people skills such as empathy to bring people along – also that women were often less protective of reputation and authority than men and ceded authority more easily." (Williams, 2013b)

In a briefing paper for managers involved in a Community for Children's Programme in South Australia (Box 5.1), the importance of many of the relationship behaviours discussed above have been consolidated into one practical model.

Box 5.1: Briefing paper for 'community for children's' programme managers

This is an extract from a briefing paper commissioned by the Australian Research Alliance for Children and Youth (ARACY), which focuses on the wellbeing of Australian young people. It is designed to offer guidance for managers and other stakeholders attempting to navigate the tensions of politics, power and complexity inherent in collaborative working. These are based on overcoming, rather than avoiding, the structural tensions. It is based on the Working Alliance Theory Model and stresses the importance of the following behaviours:

1. Investing time in developing trust by getting to know each partner, their expertise, resources and limits.
2. Openly discussing relative responsibilities, liabilities, perceived benefits, good communication and participatory decision-making.
3. Engaging any non-traditional partners through innovative and strategic approaches, assuming strength-based contributions and capacities.
4. Discussing ways of minimising or avoiding the tensions of competitive relations that can undermine local alliances or collaborations.
5. Limiting onerous reporting but maintain accountability.
6. Developing performance measures that reflect local definitions of good services and minimise constraints of upward reporting.
7. Recognising that there may be competing professional priorities and local ones, which need to be discussed and integrated.
8. Avoiding unrealistic expectations and ensure that differing priorities and obligations do not lead to competing interpretations of primary goals.

Source: This case study is taken from ARACY, 2007

Profiles of collaborating middle managers

Further evidence of the importance of managing relationships in collaborative management has been documented in my research studies. The interviewing topic guides for these research studies included an open-ended question that asked interviewees, based on a real-life example with which they were familiar, to describe a model collaborator – someone whom they considered to be a particularly effective exponent of this form of management. This generated a fascinating range of profiles, a selection of which are illustrated in Box 5.2. They substantially underscore the thrust of the preceding discussion in this chapter, and reference how all three themes identified – managing for common purpose, managing complexity and interdependency and managing relationships – are intimately connected. They interact in a complex, changing and dynamic fashion, often making it difficult to disentangle and attribute cause and effect.

Box 5.2: Profiles of collaborating middle managers

Profile 1
Being well read and prepared on topics; demonstrating knowledge from the outset and instilling confidence from other people in the room; being well networked and understanding connections; not too structured about expectations; ready to change, influenced by partners and able to cope with change quickly; not scared to change direction; being facilitative, listening and able to debate openly; ensuring a fair process and aware of potential losers.

Comment
This account refers to an effective exponent of this form of management who is able to combine relevant knowledge with an open, facilitative style of engagement that is comfortable with change and being influenced by others. In addition, there is an awareness that collaboration does not always reap equal rewards for all participants, and that this needs to be acknowledged and managed. Delicate balances have to be struck to ensure that all participants, not necessarily immediately, but over a period of time, can point to clear benefits of working together in this fashion.

Profile 2
Good communicator, listens well, not defensive; gives on occasions and not necessarily having as much back; having the foresight to see long-term goals; knowledge of own service; some understanding/being able to take on board the needs/procedures of other organisations; clear in terms of what

you both want to get out of the collaboration and what you will gain from it, even if it varies; forming networks to use in other areas.

Comment

The emphasis here is placed on securing clarity of purpose particularly over the longer term; on calculating the distribution of potential benefits between different parties; and on appreciating the frames of other organisations.

Profile 3

Open to suggestions and ideas; understanding what goes on in each organisation; the way they operate, the pressures placed on each of them, the way they plan and set priorities; to be inquisitive; to offer a level of challenge in a non-confrontational way to probe and understand; to be motivated by making stuff happen; listening and building relationships; getting to know people naturally; finding things to talk about with professional relationships spilling into social ones; building trust and giving something of yourself; negotiating and persuasion skills; helping people to understand their respective positions; their constraints and restrictions; trying to work through these to make things happen.

Comment

This account emphasises the value of empathy and understanding the world through the eyes of their partners. This is often dependent upon developing effective personal relationships and acquiring over time an appreciation of the working frames and personal lives of others. The 'person' and the 'professional' are seen as intermingled, and this person might be described as a 'frame articulator'.

Profile 4

Open, honest and saying how they feel; understanding and committed to the goal; not hiding things; not keeping power to themselves – they share it or give it to somebody else; mostly 'nice' people but you don't have to be so to be effective; more inclined to share if there is a personal element of trust and can achieve more with higher trust.

Comment

The choice of this collaborating middle manager is very much about personal characteristics, values and behaviours – about the value and potential of developing trust by being open, honest, transparent and being prepared to share and distribute power – not seek to be directive and autocratic.

Profile 5

Seeing the bigger picture and communicating it in plain English; understanding the politics – and what makes people tick; not being defensive or too subjective; needing to know the detail; solutions-focused; good negotiator and broker; selective of which battles to pick and which to lose; valuing other people; not think you are the expert in everything; having empathy and promoting two-way communication.

Comment

This choice of an effective collaborative middle manager underscores an appreciation of the complex picture of interdependencies and connections; a realisation that expertise is shared between participating managers; and that the skills of communication, negotiation and brokering are vital in being able to develop future actions.

Profile 6

Being evangelical to get the message out and explain why there needs to be change and collaboration; being a mediator and negotiator – honest broker – having strength in the knowledge of key issues – understanding the political playing field – bringing things together – understanding the different motivations of people in different organisations – and offering solutions and negotiating shared outcomes – being an 'extrapreneur'.

Comment

This profile majors on collaboration and its association with change and the ability to engage in innovative, creative and entrepreneurial processes. Understanding politics and the multiple motivations of partners which they are garnering in pursuit of solutions and making things happen. The reference to being 'evangelical' is interesting because it reflects the need for a degree of charisma to mobilise and sustain collaborative action often through an elongated and tortuous process.

A dominant theme from these and other profiles is summarised in the conclusion by O'Leary and Bingham (2007: 6) that: 'the most important skills needed for today's managers are negotiation, bargaining, collaborative problem solving, conflict management, and conflict resolution. Yet many public managers find themselves ill-equipped for management in a shared-power world.' These authors' guide to resolving conflicts in collaborative networks is a very helpful framework for addressing this problem, based on the idea that:

> members should invest in preparation, bring an open mind to network meetings, and brainstorm options collaboratively with other network members. This means identifying their own and their organisation's interests and needs in advance, as well as researching and thinking about the other parties' interests and needs prior to negotiating. It also means focusing on creative solutions that address the procedural, substantive, and relationship (or psychological) needs of all the parties involved. (O'Leary and Bingham, 2007: 35)

Above all, it is the human face of collaborative working that is constantly underscored by practitioners, policy makers and managers engaged in conversations about this form of governance, and as Getha-Taylor (2008: 118) reflects, 'the most basic and critical factor of collaboration is interpersonal understanding, which only comes through time and experience'. Unquestionably, structural determinants and the imposition or configuration of boundaries will influence the appetite for, and design and delivery of, collaboration, but agency makes it happen, and that agency involves actors working together to manage the complex mechanisms and processes of collaboration. This is rooted in relationships – an inextricable mixture of personal and professional exchanges, cemented through trust, painstakingly cultivated, constantly being evaluated, but inherently fragile and exposed to the uncontrolled external shocks of a dynamic and volatile policy and political environment.

Key points of learning

- The essence of working effectively in collaboration is widely considered to be dependent upon **developing and sustaining relationships** with a diverse set of stakeholders and interests – building social capital and personal networks to design and deliver collaborative outcomes.
- The focus on **cultivating personal and professional relationships** is critical in being able to manage the cross-boundary challenges that originate from diverse organisations, sectors, cultures, professions and accountabilities.
- Working with middle managers in other organisations over a **sustained period of time** especially on a face to face basis either individually or at meetings, coupled with telephone conversations and email exchanges is considered to be the best way of building personal and professional relationships.
- **Trust** is universally considered to be at the heart of managing personal and professional relationships – although its understanding is open to a variety of interpretations – based on calculative, value or norm-based and common cognition models. Although trust is often considered to occur at a personal level, it can be manifested at a systems level in the form of a shared history of partnership working between organisations in a particular locality or policy area.
- **Trust** can sometimes be considered as 'insincere' – just a façade for another means of power.
- There is a school of thought that suggests that middle managers need to reflect **extrovert personalities** – to be sociable, engaging, confident, self-assured and comfortable around people from different backgrounds. This may be an appropriate style for some, but for others, the sincerity of their inter-personal relationships can be legitimately demonstrated through other behaviours and actions.
- **Relationship building** is valuable in being able to make sense of the connectivity of policy areas and collaborative opportunities, and networking accelerates joint learning and knowledge management with colleagues from other organisations that can be used to shape the ongoing

collaborative process, but also be transferred and used for the benefit of their own organisations.

Suggested further reading

ARACY (Australian Research Alliance for Children and Youth) (2007) *The Impact of Power and Politics in a Complex Environment*, Canberra: ARACY

Lane, C. and Bachmann, R. (1998) *Trust In and Between Organisations*, Oxford: Oxford University Press

Oomsels, P. and Bouckaert, G. (2014) 'Studying interorganisational trust in public administration', *Public Performance and Management Review*, Vol. 37 (4), pp. 577–604

6

Managing within and between organisations

Managing interorganisational networks is unquestionably a difficult job. At the least, it is most certainly a different job that requires different skills.

(Kettl, 2006: 16)

This chapter explores some of the existing evidence and contested positions around the contrasts and comparisons between managing within the confines of organisations, as opposed to managing between organisations in forms of collaboration. Researchers and practitioners come to various conclusions on the key questions relating to the extent to which managing in collaborative forms of governance requires a unique form of management or not, and if so, the skills and competencies middle managers need to be effective in this form of management. Figure 6.1 suggests that these can be crudely mapped across a spectrum of positions from those who see it as broadly the same, those who judge it to be not quite the same, and those who see it as definitely different.

The school of thought that considers that management in the two forms of governance is different, takes the view that this stems from broadly contextual reasons relating to the form, structure and purposes inherent in the respective contexts. The consequence being that the management and behaviour of middle managers needs to be different. O'Toole and Meir (2010: 324) underscore this perspective in their observation that:

inducements to and constraints inhibiting cooperation across organisational boundaries in networked and collaborative settings are different from – and typically more challenging than – generating successful cooperative implementation via unified organisations. Authority is typically weaker in interorganisational situations, and encouragement toward cooperation must perforce rely less on established communication channels, routines, and shared worldviews than it does within hierarchical agencies.

The broad conclusions of my own research also consider that the central concerns and activities of management in each of the respective settings are fundamentally different, primarily because of the focus of management in the respective forms as illustrated in Figure 6.2. Middle manager's tasks and functions within their organisations revolve around human resource management and financial budgeting set within the

Figure 6.1: Spectrum of positions on management within and between organisations

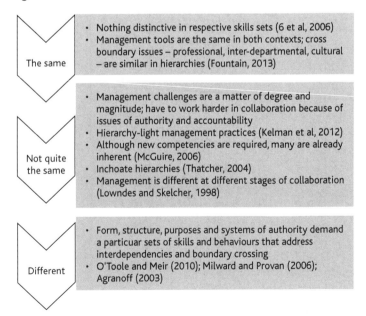

The same
- Nothing distinctive in respective skills sets (6 et al, 2006)
- Management tools are the same in both contexts; cross boundary issues – professional, inter-departmental, cultural – are similar in hierarchies (Fountain, 2013)

Not quite the same
- Management challenges are a matter of degree and magnitude; have to work harder in collaboration because of issues of authority and accountability
- Hierarchy-light management practices (Kelman et al, 2012)
- Although new competencies are required, many are already inherent (McGuire, 2006)
- Inchoate hierarchies (Thatcher, 2004)
- Management is different at different stages of collaboration (Lowndes and Skelcher, 1998)

Different
- Form, structure, purposes and systems of authority demand a particuar sets of skills and behaviours that address interdependencies and boundary crossing
- O'Toole and Meir (2010); Milward and Provan (2006); Agranoff (2003)

Figure 6.2: Managing within and between organisations

Managing within organisations
People
Budgets
Functions

Managing between organisations
Common purpose
Interdependencies
Relationships

boundaries of defined professionally based departments. In public service agencies, purposes and roles are often defined by statute, systems of accountability and performance management are prescribed through hierarchical structures, and power relationships and status are widely acknowledged. Admittedly, the move towards more networked forms of organisation and the need for corporate and inter-departmental planning presents new challenges for middle managers, and perhaps begins to demand management behaviours and skills more familiar to collaborative settings. However, the fundamentals and principles of a single organisation remain. In contrast, within collaborative frameworks, the management focus must engage in the negotiation of common purpose in highly interdependent and complex settings requiring sensitive and well-developed relationship skills and abilities. Within organisations, middle managers can largely direct the course of action through their control over staff and budgets, protected by the cushion of the bureaucracy. Size of budget, number of staff and span of responsibilities are the measures of a middle manager's status. Not so in collaborative arenas; lots of things are up for grabs, to be contested and negotiated in the search for benefits that can only be released by agencies working together. The value of a collaborative middle manager derives from other avenues as explored in the previous three chapters, requiring a different focus from those involved in managing within organisations. Agency encompasses power relationships that have to be more facilitative and empowering with underlying management skills and behaviours that reflect a proven appreciation of managing relationships.

Network management, policy network and collaborative public management perspectives (Kickert et al, 1997; Agranoff, 2007; Goldsmith and Eggers, 2004; O'Leary and Bingham, 2009) reflect the need to adapt to the demands and realities of a highly interdependent environment where crossing boundaries becomes the mainstream. This requires particular skill sets, approaches and behaviours set out in previous chapters. Milward and Provan (2006: 11) are clear on this point in their assertion that:

> networks are quite different from organisational hierarchies. In particular, networks are generally collaborative, non-bureaucratic structures, involving autonomous organisations that are often responsive to a broad range of non-governmental stakeholders, while also working in interdependent ways with both government and other network providers. Thus, effective network management requires skills and development of coordinating structures that are not the same as those that might be effective for managing individual organisations.

Agranoff (2003) is on the same page with his view that working in a network is quite different for most managers who are otherwise largely preoccupied with tasks and functions within their own organisations. The main difference is that, in a network, 'all managers face a nonhierarchical self-organizing situation where jointly agreed focus and purpose prevails' (Agranoff, 2003: 14). He does, however, recognise one exception to this dichotomy in the shape of boundary spanners or managers in dedicated liaison roles, whose: 'inside and outside work is in many ways similar as they reach across and represent their program as full-time partner or network participant. But even the boundary spanner who does different work is within a hierarchy with standard management processes as he/she communicates with the home organisation.'

A competing school of thought argues, however, that these skills and behaviours are equally applicable within organisations, particularly those that are highly fragmented by profession, division, department and geography. Fountain (2013) articulates this position admirably by arguing that management practices and behaviours are broadly similar whether a manager is working within or between organisations. She points to the hierarchical design of many cross-agency collaborations and their use of formal roles, structures and coordinating mechanisms, all recognisable in traditional hierarchical organisations. Furthermore, she concedes that a source of variance may lie in the particular use of indirect management skills such as persuasion, negotiation and conflict management in collaborative working, but argues that these may indeed be necessary but ultimately not sufficient in themselves. This is because in addition to these collaborative management skills:

> interagency projects require rigorous, systematic management systems and processes. Ultimately, government executives and managers working across boundaries have to develop and sustain authority, legitimacy, and credibility across jurisdictions and often across cultures. What holds the actors together in a network are perceptions that joint gains will be produced that will exceed the costs of forgoing some measure of agency autonomy. (Fountain, 2013: 18)

Fountain does appreciate the demanding nature of working with other agencies because of the size, complexity and interdependent nature of collaborative arrangements. This entails extra communication and high transaction costs to negotiate legitimacy and share resources and expertise, together with a collaborative management skills set comprising:

- an understanding of, and ability to work strategically within the institutional environment;
- the development and use of interpersonal skills to build strong professional relationships and teams;
- the ability to build capacity across boundaries through rigorous structures and processes with the extra commitment and coordination required to work across agency boundaries.

Fountain (2013) appears to be arguing, therefore, that collaborative management is a bit like inter-departmental management, but middle managers have to work harder because the challenges are more difficult. The point she makes about many collaborations ultimately having to design structures and coordinating mechanisms more familiar to single organisations is an interesting one, because it resonates with the argument that the design and planning stages of collaborative efforts are often characterised by more flexible arrangements, but when it comes to implementation and delivery, much more formal structures need to be installed to clarify who does what, and who is accountable for delivery. Kelman et al (2012: 624), drawing on research evidence from Crime and Disorder Partnerships in Britain, come to a broadly similar conclusion to Fountain in their assertion that: 'effective collaboration management uses tools to manage *any* organisation: being a good *collaboration* manager involves *good management, period*'. Expanding on this general conclusion, they further conclude that:

- 'When a collaboration succeeds in improving performance, it does so because managers have used general management tools in circumstances favorable to collaboration success.'
- 'In situations where it makes sense to have a collaboration, managers should prioritize hierarchy-light practices'. Hierarchy-light practices include, monitoring mechanisms to ensure that partner organisations deliver on their commitments; dealing with 'blockages' to sort out problems and issues; and setting in place performance management measures – all three of which are central roles of the manager operating in classical hierarchies.
- 'Furthermore, managing a collaboration often works better where *single agencies work better*, so if you want collaborations among agencies to succeed, you need to worry about the health of *individual agencies*.'

Again, Agranoff (2006: 57) is in similar territory with his view that: 'networks are different from organisations but not completely different' and that: 'lateral connections seem to overlay the hierarchy rather than act as a replacement for them'. McGuire (2006: 39) also supports this broad view that there are similarities between the skill demands of collaborative management and those of managing single organisations. He argues that although new competencies are needed for collaboration, some of these are already inherent in middle managers working in hierarchical organisations, including communication among staff, inclusive strategic management and planning, mechanisms to organise and disseminate information and conflict resolution. Also, 'managers in both contexts influence rules and structure daily. The same principle and application apply both to networks and hierarchies: If the structure does not fit the task, performance will suffer.'

6 et al (2006: 157) conclude that:

> nothing in the boundary spanning literature shows that there is anything particularly distinctive either about the activities or about the skill sets of boundary spanners working between organisations when compared, for example, with colleagues working between departments within an organisation. Essentially, the same processes of initiation, negotiation, diplomacy, problem-solving and strategic development – and the same tact, ability to move between accountabilities, energy to motivate others etc. – are required in both settings.

They do concede, however, that there may be some differences between the two contexts that may be important but only to a degree, and these relate to scope for selection, structures, boundaries and accountability. Although it is often easy to underestimate the difficulties many middle managers encounter when attempting to mediate/negotiate across professional, legal, cultural and personal boundaries that exist within organisations.

Thatcher (2004) takes the view, on the basis of his research in the field of community safety that 'partnerships' are not unique new institutional forms but new organisations in the process of development, and that

> if the forces that led to formalization in the Community Safety Initiative are common ones, then there may be many partnerships that operate not like something completely different from markets and hierarchies but at least partly like inchoate hierarchies – like efforts to develop new organizations in the spaces between those that already exist. (Thatcher, 2004: 92)

This view is somewhat at odds with other researchers who promote a network approach and who: 'share the view that partnerships are best understood as social interactions outside of a structured hierarchy – that is, that partnerships are governed by the dynamics of informal social cooperation rather than the dynamics of action within formal organisations' (Thatcher, 2004: 93). Here, the management of partnerships emphasise trust building as the primary mechanism for gluing interests together, rather than designing structures that foreground role definitions, accountability structures and mechanisms for arbitration.

Thatcher's research (2004) found that: 'many partnerships remain partly stuck in network form as inchoate hierarchies rather than fully developed organisations'; that collaborative action in unstructured situations was a problem; and that the projects he examined exhibited evidence of culture and structure in their development rules, norms, systems and roles. Interestingly, this was viewed partly in response to the isolationist roles of whom he termed the 'guerillas of the bureaucracy' or boundary spanners who found it difficult to resolve the conflicting forces of their home organisations and the partnerships, together with the perennial problems of accountability. The broad conclusion of this research was that: 'these interorganisational collaborations cannot be described solely in terms of reciprocal communication and exchange between independent actors; the parties eventually interacted in a more structured context'; that 'partnership is usefully understood as an inchoate organisation rather than (or in addition to) something altogether different from hierarchical organisation'; and that: 'on the practical side, it suggests that the management of partnerships can and perhaps should draw on many conventional managerial nostrums developed with hierarchical organisations in mind' (Thatcher, 2004: 122). Last, Thatcher (2004) suggests that: 'networks and hierarchies might be viewed as stages in a historical sequence in which networking strategies are used to *establish* the hierarchical structures within which action takes place thereafter' (Thatcher, 2004: 123). This resonates with stagist models of partnerships such as the life cycle model expounded by Lowndes and Skelcher (1998). They link stages in the development of partnerships to different modes of governance. So, the early stages of formation that emphasise informality, networking and exploration are characterised by network governance; the partnership creation and consolidation stage is more hierarchical in nature based on efforts to formalise arrangements through systems and structures; and the delivery and implementation stages might involve conventional public service delivery but also market contractual conditions. The implication of this model is that the management of partnerships will need to reflect different modes of governance at different stages.

My research (Williams, 2017) involving middle managers concluded that it was not possible to reach any definitive consensus on whether managing internally was different to managing in collaboration. The middle managers interviewed in the various research studies took various positions on this matter which could be mapped along a continuum – at one end, from there being a: 'discernible difference between the two because internally you have the choice of being directive or collaborative, but in collaboration, you have no option but to adopt a collaborative approach' to those who, while recognising that there were different challenges posed by working in collaborative arenas, did not consider that they demanded management approaches and skills that were in any way different to their normal within organisation practices. One middle manager asserted that: 'management styles between the respective modes does not materially differ – it is contingent on the context and issue', and in a broadly similar vein, another manager concluded that: 'the same skills were necessary for both but needed to be used in a slightly different way'. For instance, collaboration brought to the forefront the need for particular skills such negotiation, consensus seeking and networking. At the other end of the continuum, some middle managers, admittedly in the minority, agreed that collaboration demanded a distinct set of management approaches and skills.

Box 6.1: Middle manager's attitudes to managing in collaboration

Research study

Views of middle managers in a South Wales local council

Collaborative settings were described as: "more complex to deal with particularly with the greater number of partners and the consequent effect on dynamics and relationships". They were seen to be: "particularly challenging and different" because of different cultures and decision-making frameworks. For instance, reference was made to the contrast between the Local Health Board and the council – the former having command and control type structures and less distributed decision-making powers for senior managers than their counterparts in the council, particularly in terms of financial matters. A selection of views included the following:

- "Management is different but no different skills are required."
- "Some management styles are transferable and applicable to both inside and outside organisations – I have a collaborative management style – gain views and listen to colleagues – patience is important – must understand how other people operate in their authorities – understanding what other people are dealing with – talking and listening to them – communicating."
- "Managing is not different – you can't be schizophrenic – you should have a clear set of outcomes to achieve and deliver on these – it doesn't matter who you work with – clarity on outcomes and monitoring – I don't view the world differently and act differently – no special skills are necessary – bringing people together from different disciplines within or outside is the most important."
- "I don't adopt a different style/approach in different settings."

Source: Williams, 2017

If there was a tendency towards consensus from the evidence of this study, it would be that middle managers needed to possess a generic set of skills and competencies that they then deployed in suitable combinations and permutations depending upon the circumstances, context and challenges facing them – departmentally, inter-departmentally or in collaboration. The ability to do this would require considerable sensitivity and judgement, would be enhanced through experience of these different situations, but may be fraught with danger if used inappropriately or inconsistently.

Similar questions to the ones posed here in relation to management, can be directed to leadership. What is leadership in collaborative settings and what behaviours characterise leaders, and how does leadership in collaboration differ from leadership in single-agency contexts, if at all? Earlier chapters set out a number of models that promote a distinctive character to leadership for collaboration – models that emphasise relationship building, understanding complexity, promoting learning and innovation and being underpinned by shared and distributed leadership processes. There are, inevitably, many nuances in the research of the numerous proponents of these leadership models, as well as on the questions posed above. Silvia and McGuire (2010) have tackled these questions head-on using a large sample of actors involved in emergency management, and analysing their responses to 35 leadership behaviours. They used the notion of integrative leadership to capture the predominant approach in networks where leaders focus on sharing leadership and information, treating members as equals; building trust; and looking to identify resources and stakeholders. But conversely, such leaders focus less on tasks, setting expectations and work scheduling. Broadly, they found that people-orientated behaviours appeared to be more central to the leader operating in networks as compared to the task-orientated behavioural focus of working within agencies. Also, there were some similarities between network-level behaviour and single-agency behaviour, mainly among the organisation-oriented behaviours, such as identifying resources, encouraging support from stakeholders and identifying stakeholders.

Dickinson and Carey (2016: 54) conclude that: 'there may be nothing unique to collaboration regarding the leadership styles and skills that facilitate their success; rather, the difference may lie in the emphasis on particular elements of a more generic leadership model and in the specific contexts – and the challenges therein – within which they are deployed'. The practice of leadership, then, is contingent on the situation, the context, the policy and political environment and the challenges a leader faces irrespective of whether this is intra or inter-organisational. A leader has a toolbox of skills, competencies and abilities, underpinned by a set of personality traits from which to select. Some will be more or less appropriate or effective at any one time.

Managing accountabilities

A significant fault line between managing within and between organisations lies in the matter of accountability. In the normal course of management, they are subject to a wide range of possible sources of accountability as detailed by Lynn (2006) and illustrated in Table 6.1 – statutory and legal duties, professional bodies, democratic mechanisms and public service values. But managing in collaboration increases this and exacerbates the potential for conflict and tension between them.

In my research (Williams, 2017), the issue of accountability was one that generated considerable concern among middle managers. Interviewees were asked their opinions on two questions when they were managing in collaborative settings: 'Who are you accountable to – the council, the user, the collaboration, or your profession?' and 'Do you accept single or joint accountability for services that you jointly design and delivery with other agencies?' The responses were varied. One interviewee rephrased the dilemma as: "Who are you batting for – the council or the greater good?" Another interviewee commented that: "accountability can cause tensions – you must express different loyalties; you must be loyal to your council because you are in a collaborative to improve things for your organisation; organisational self-interest is important; but some collaborations don't generate huge benefits for us but we co-

Table 6.1: Mechanisms of accountability

Executive authority	• Accepted systems of moral value e.g. public service ethos, codes of ethics • Professionalism and expertise e.g. certified by accredited bodies • Performance targets, balanced scorecards, evaluations • Incentives e.g. rewards for performance
Legislative authority	• Detailed legislative prescription which limits discretion of managers • Monitoring provisions of legislation • Freedom of information and financial disclosures • Legislated performance goals and indicators • Ombudsman and inspectorates
Legal authority	• Codes of legally enforceable rules • Liability of public officials in common law • Judicial review • Separation of government powers
Popular authority	• Constitutionally established elections and referenda • Participatory democracy mechanisms

Source: Based on Lynn, 2006: 139

operate for the greater good". Another referred to having: "to flip flop between various interests" requiring experience to balance the risks with the benefits.

Some interviewees were concerned about the risks involved in "handing over the delivery of certain services to other agencies" while retaining statutory accountability for them. This was seen as an area of tension that demanded sensitive management supported by effective governance frameworks. The need for some kind of formalisation in terms of agreements, protocols or contracts was considered to be especially important in dealing with the private sector because it was not part of a public sector ethos – "it was outside the local government family – for example around forms of procurement". This reinforces the argument posited previously about the need to design robust accountability and performance management frameworks akin to single agencies to ensure clarification and commitment over who does what, because trust-based systems are insufficient in themselves to instil reliability and transparency.

Balancing organisational and collaborative roles

Perhaps the differences between managing within and between organisations are cast into particularly sharp focus in terms of the challenges, sensitivities and tensions that are necessary to balance the organisational and collaborative roles of middle managers. Agranoff (2003: 28) maintains that:

> to be an effective network participant, one must balance the dualism of agency and collective concerns. As a formal or informal boundary spanner, one must first of all know your own agency, its programs, administrators, technologies, funding bases, regulations, and so on. This requires a constant flow of communication within the home agency. In this sense the boundary spanning activity extends to intraorganisational as well as interorganisational domains.

In my research (Williams, 2017) middle managers offered a number of perspectives on their role in general, and the tensions and accountabilities stemming from managing both within and between organisations. A number of managers referred to the pressures on middle managers having to service collaborative structures and relationships, and balancing these with the daily internal organisational burdens. The bureaucracy of 'collaborative machinery' was often considered to be onerous in terms of staff, facilities, resources and time. This perception prevails in particular where collaborative management is seen as an 'added on' responsibility rather than one that is considered to be an integral part of a middle manager's job description and normal duties.

Undoubtedly, there was a clear recognition that this cadre of management was powerfully placed to influence the course of collaboration and its implications for their organisations, positively or negatively, particularly through their mediation of relationships between the top of the organisation and the staff delivering frontline services. Research by Agranoff (2003) emphasises the positional importance of middle managers making these links upwards and downwards, and their catalytic role in providing both technical and organising energy to sustain the process within their agencies, so helping to deliver the work of networks. He suggests that these middle managers 'become involved in developing joint information events and activities, and engage extensively in information sharing, are at meetings to access information and emerging technologies, and communicate the networks' concerns with their home agencies' (Agranoff, 2013: 18). This championing role is important because it signals to sometimes-reluctant members of their home organisations that working in collaboration is both legitimate and rewarding.

There was reference in my research to 'the middle management sponge' that represented a significant obstacle to collaborative working because of the need for the preservation of status, control, turf, finance and professional identity. The personal and career prospects of middle managers were not often linked to collaboration, and some viewed it as a direct threat to their power bases as reported by one middle manager in the following terms: "There are personal and career agendas with middle managers – collaboration can be a threat because of giving up power and resources – some people shut down and are not engaged." Collaboration is an inherently riskier endeavour than working within organisations, and one that some middle managers were neither comfortable with, nor experienced in. One suggestion was that as managers proceed through the organisational hierarchy they acquire "different priorities and lose their service user focus as they go higher up the ladder". These are strong messages that need to be taken on board by organisations that are committed to working in collaboration. They have clear implications for the training and development of middle managers as well as for systems of reward and incentives.

Key points of learning

- There are **contested positions around the contrasts and comparisons** between managing within organisations, as opposed to managing between organisations in forms of collaboration.

- **One school of thought** argues that for broadly contextual reasons relating to the form, structure and purposes of collaboration, management and the behaviour of middle managers needs to be different. This requires particular skill sets, approaches and behaviours particularly around the core task of managing common purpose, appreciating complexity and interdependencies, and managing relationships.

- **An alternative school of thought** argues that management skills and behaviours are equally applicable within and between organisations, particularly those that are highly fragmented by professional, division, department and geography and demand considerable inter-departmental and corporate working.

- It might be argued that middle managers **need to possess a generic set of skills and competencies** that they then deploy in suitable combinations and permutations depending upon the circumstances, context and challenges facing them – departmentally, inter-departmentally or in collaboration.

- **Lines of accountability** may represent a significant fault line between managing within and between organisations. The range of accountabilities is increased in collaborative settings and constitutes significant tensions and balances.

- These are reinforced in the **tensions** created by the balances middle managers have to make in their collaborative and organisational roles. Career progression and systems of reward are geared to favouring allegiance to the home organisation.

Suggested further reading

Fountain, J. (2013) *Implementing Cross-Agency Collaboration: A Guide for Federal Managers*, Washington, DC: IBM Centre for Business of Government

McGuire, M. (2006) 'Collaborative public management: Assessing what we know and how we know it', *Public Administration Review*, Vol. 66 (Special Issue), pp. 33–43

7

Implications for policy, practice and learning

Even those career executives who have a singular agency focus (and there will always be some) will have to be able to demonstrate the ability to lead across boundaries as the things government does become more and more interconnected, co-produced, and net-centric. (National Academy of Public Administration, 2007: 303)

The factors and determinants that shape and influence the course of collaboration are highly complex and interrelated. They are nested in a multifaceted and tangled web consisting of contextual, governance and agential elements – context shaped by institutional and structural factors, legislative arrangements and statutory duties, financial regimes, broader economic and social drivers, and local history of collaboration; governance moulded through culture, decision-making structures, accountability and performance management frameworks, and role and purpose; agency manifested through leadership, professionalism, experience and personal characteristics of public leaders, practitioners, politicians and managers.

The focus of this book lies squarely on the role and contribution of 'middle managers' in this mosaic of collaborative machinery. Previous chapters have examined some of the theories and research available on this subject, and presented additional insights particularly from my own research studies in this area. This chapter responds to the 'so what does this mean for policy and practice' question. What lessons can policy makers

Figure 7.1: Factors influencing collaborative working

and practitioners take from this analysis to help shape the design and delivery of future collaborative interventions, and how might it inform the progress and trajectory of existing management practice? In particular, it explores some of the implications of this book for learning – for the education, training and development of middle managers. As a general statement, the thrust of middle management training and development is still heavily biased towards intra-organisational management and not managing in collaboration. This might be considered somewhat perverse given the exponential growth of collaborative working which is likely to be sustained into the future. A report of the National Academy of Public Administration (2007: 273) was stark in its message that:

> The reality is that...senior executives (SES members and otherwise) are almost exclusively agency-centric in skill set and mindset, as functionally and organizationally stove-piped as the government itself. Most have remained in the same agency for their entire careers, often promoted for their technical skills and never venturing across (much less out of) the Federal enterprise to broaden their experience or their expertise. The result: few are equipped to lead the whole-of-government enterprise.

Over ten years later, the situation here and elsewhere has arguably not altered significantly. Why is it that managing in collaboration still fails to tip the balance away from managing within organisations, and attract the necessary training and development it deserves? Does the view that managing in collaboration is not sufficiently different from managing within organisations prevail as the perceived wisdom? Does experience of collaborative working substitute for formal training and development, or to be effective, does it require the identification, training and development in specific skills and competencies? Can collaborative management acquire the same recognition as management in single organisations?

Again, drawing on the excellent report of the National Academy of Public Administration (2007), it concludes that the twenty-first century leader faces new and more complex competency requirements that need to replace the traditional supervision and management focus. Box 7.1 outlines the skills and abilities that are necessary, not just for top level executives, but for all team leaders, first-line supervisors and middle managers.

Box 7.1: Skills and abilities for the twenty-first century leader

1. Cognitive ability, both raw intellectual horsepower and mental agility;
2. strategic thinking skills, especially regarding application of technology to business strategy and operations;
3. analytical ability, especially the ability to sort through myriad information sources and focus on the most relevant data aspects;
4. the ability to make sound decisions in an environment of ambiguity and uncertainty;
5. the ability to employ various management styles in a diverse environment that includes three or four generations and cultures in the workplace at once, each dealing with work–life balance issues;
6. the ability to lead people not physically co-located with the manager, requiring new approaches to assigning work, communicating expectations, monitoring work and assessing performance;

7. the ability to lead a contingent or blended workforce of contractors, permanent and temporary personnel, US and local national employees, military, public health service;
8. the ability to apply matrix management by building teams and utilising personnel for their individual skills notwithstanding their permanent assignment to another organisation.

Source: National Academy of Public Administration, 2007: 303

It rejects the distinction that is often made between leaders and managers and the competencies that each should possess, and argues that:

> What is essential, though, is to have leaders at all levels who can provide leadership and effective management. Individuals are needed who can focus on vision and detail; who can execute as well as plan; who can understand and use all resources – human, financial, information and technological; who can take and manage risks; who can reward and discipline; who know how to achieve results, yet maintain integrity and values, within a system of laws, regulations and principles; and who work toward common goals with diverse individuals and varied groups including customers, employees, labor unions, professional associations, academic institutions, law makers, regulators, and contractors. (National Academy of Public Administration, 2004: 17–18)

The implications of this discussion for policy and practice in cross-boundary work again reinforces the need to ensure that the actors involved in this activity are suitably trained and developed to discharge this form of management. There is a tendency to assume that a proven ability in managing intra-organisationally is a sufficient passport to gain entry to cross-boundary management. However, there is compelling evidence to suggest that this is a false premise and counterproductive to effective cooperative behaviours.

Collaborative roles, job performance and competencies

The roles of middle managers operating in spheres of collaboration are diverse, and broadly they are of two types. One involves the middle managers who have a dedicated job role to manage in multi-agency/cross-sector settings. These have been referred to as 'boundary spanners' (Williams, 2012a) and occupy posts in various policy areas, committing much of their time to the servicing, coordination and planning of inter-organisational initiatives. These are relatively few in number compared with the bulk of other middle managers who devote varying amounts of time and effort to collaborative activities – in other words it is part of a mainstream job role, and variously considered to be integral or bolted-on!

Although the context of this book is public sector, lessons from the private sector can be valuable. For instance, Floyd and Wooldridge (1994) have examined the role of middle managers in creating competitive advantage in a context where organisational boundaries are increasingly blurred because of the growth of networks between suppliers, customers and competitors. They suggest that specific middle managers need to be identified, trained and developed to operate in this environment with boundary spanning experience, a strategic mindset and teamwork skills. The interesting point is that this might result in a re-engineering of the organisation as a whole to enable it to better respond to the market and environment. By the same token, contemporary public service agencies might question whether a review of the role of middle managers in the light of the demands of collaboration could result in a re-structuring or re-engineering of the organisation as a whole. And if so, how?

Box 7.2: Principles for developing the role of middle managers in pursuit of competitive advantage

1. Recognise the link between middle management, core capability and competitive advantage. Most fundamentally, re-engineering should occur with an awareness of the link between middle management and firm competitiveness.

2. Identify middle managers with the appropriate skills, experiences and potential to thrive within the new organisation: Our research shows the importance of boundary spanning experience as one criterion for discriminating among middle managers. Another consideration is that middle management in the reengineered organisation requires a strategic mindset and teamwork skills.

3. Develop a better understanding of desired roles within the organisation: for reengineering to pay off, top managers need to analyse the changed role of middle management and begin to develop it within the organisation.

4. Redesign the organisation to leverage the knowledge and skills of a selected set of middle managers and encourage their influence on strategic priorities. Organisational boundaries are becoming increasingly fuzzy as networks of suppliers, customers, and competitors are formed to cope with enormously complex and demanding circumstances. Organisations want to capture the influence of middle managers who relate to the market and technological environments. In order to open up the organisation to environmental influence, boundary-spanning middle managers should become the owners of product development, order fulfilment, and other key business processes. The need for power shifts from functional to process leadership.

5. Renegotiate the 'psychological contract' by committing to the ongoing involvement of middle management in the strategy-making process.

Source: Floyd and Wooldridge, 1994

The question about what makes people effective in particular job roles is the subject of considerable interest and literature. Hirsch and Strebler (1994) refer to 'skill languages' to describe the fashionable methodologies used to describe the 'ideal manager'. These include studies of managerial activities and roles; exercises where lists of activities and roles are matched with desirable skills and personal attributes; knowledge-based profiles; expressions of output and performance; and more recently, the notion of competence. Unsurprisingly, the debate about the appropriateness of each language is contested. One view argues that there is no proven methodology for linking activities and roles with skills and attributes, rather it is preferable to 'assess performance in activities directly than to believe we can accurately assess personal attributes' (Hirsh and Bevan, 1988: 18). Some of the literature attempts to search for a distinction between skills and personal attributes but any differentiation is confused by the frequent use of other terms such as 'abilities', 'traits', 'aptitudes', and 'disposition' to mean the same or sometimes different things. One possible clear distinction lies in the difference between the possession of a particular set of skills and the execution in practice. Here, the determinants of the quality of execution may be influenced by underlying personal attributes relating to personality, attitudes and cognitive abilities. Some researchers (Katz, 1974) reject the personality trait route in favour of a skills-based approach where skills are abilities that can be developed, not necessarily inborn, and can be technical, human and conceptual in type.

One popular method that avoids making distinctions between skills, abilities and traits lies in the notion of competence and job performance. Boyatzis (1982: 21) defines a job competency as: 'an underlying characteristic of a person in that it may be a motive, trait, skill, aspect of one's self-image or social role, or a body of knowledge which he or she uses'. He develops a model consisting of three elements – the demands of the job (tasks, functional requirements and roles); the organisational environment (context and culture); and an individual's competencies. The competency approach has gained, and continues to attract, considerable traction but it is not without its detractors, such as Woodruffe (1992: 16) who comments that: 'it often seems to be used as an umbrella term to cover almost anything that might directly or indirectly affect job performance'. He takes a narrower view of the notion in his definition that: 'it is a set of behaviour patterns that the incumbent needs to bring to a position in order to perform its tasks and functions with competence' or 'behavioral repertoires that some people carry out better than others' (p. 17). This interpretation suggests that competency is about observable behaviour; that there is a need to distinguish between competence and competency; and that competencies should not be confused with technical skills and knowledge to do the job. Rather, they deal with the behaviours people need to do the job effectively and not the job per se. The main problem with this approach is that competencies are considered to be closely associated with, or determined by, personal qualities, traits and general disposition or the personality of the individual. This then risks being embroiled in the highly contested terrain of notions of personality with fundamentally opposing schools of thought on the subject from trait theorists and cognitive psychologists. This might appear to be a rather sterile discussion but it has practical implications on the influence of personality and raises the question of how far it is possible to train and develop people – in the present case, middle managers – in particular competencies relevant to managing in collaboration, and how far behaviour and effectiveness may be limited by their personality characteristics. Referring back to the discussion in previous chapters, there was feedback from many research interviewees commenting upon the appropriateness of a particular person's personality in relation to his/her ability to work in collaborative settings.

The work on competency frameworks is extensive in relation to leadership and management in general. Some look to identify generic competencies; others cluster and classify them into different groupings; and some attempt to make distinctions between competencies, for instance, hard and soft competencies (Jacobs, 1989; Boyatzis, 1982) with threshold competencies (those that are basic to do the job) and performance competencies (those that differentiate between levels of performance). There are numerous techniques available for identifying job competencies and a battery of methods for assessing performance against them based on analogous, analytical and reputational approaches. In summary, what one would expect from a realistic framework is one that is based on:

- what the job involves in relation to activities, tasks and roles;
- what the person can do which refers to skills and competencies;
- what the person achieves which relates to output and performance;

- what the person is in terms of intellect, personality and attitudes;
- what the person knows in relation to knowledge and experience.

Taking the previous discussion into account and noting the questions above, the following selection of competency frameworks about managing in collaboration are very useful, but need to be treated with some care.

Getha-Taylor (2008) is among the first to recognise the importance of translating the notion of collaborative management or boundary spanning into a formal set of skills and capabilities for managers. An explicit recognition of such skills allows educators and trainers to consider how these might be operationalised in formal and informal developmental programmes. She acknowledges the work of researchers such as Goldsmith and Eggers (2004), Chrislip and Larson (1994) and Bardach (1998) before undertaking a research study to distill collaborative competencies that are 'differentiating competencies, or those competencies that distinguish superior performers from average performers' (Getha-Taylor, 2008: 105). The findings from her research conclude that the most significant competencies for collaborative effectiveness are:

- interpersonal understanding including empathy and motivation;
- teamwork and cooperation including inclusivity, conflict resolution and altruism in resource sharing;
- team leadership including bridging diversity and creating a line of sight.

This type of approach has been embraced by a number of researchers and studies. The ARACY (2013a) factsheet is set in the context of cross-sector collaboration focusing on children and youth in Australia and offers a summary of core competencies/capabilities and characteristics. Table 7.1 specifies a rather daunting list under four headings of getting things done, analysis and planning, driving the process, and personal attributes.

Table 7.1: Core collaboration competences/capabilities and characteristics

Getting things done through others	• Communication skills • Relationship skills • Build and maintain • Nurturing • Leadership skills • Process catalyst • Group process skills • Change management skills • Negotiation skills • Deal constructively with conflict
Analysis and planning	• Listening and learning • Problem assessment • Strategic planning • Strategic relationship building • Work planning • Performance measurement and evaluation • Alignment of top down and bottom up processes
Driving the process	• Vision setting • Resources • Linking and levering relationships • Getting 'buy-in' from members • Energise and mobilise • Building coalitions • Modelling elaborator practice • Community building • Managing relationships/expectations • Assignment of tasks and people
Personal attributes	• Able to 'read' interactions and exchanges • Trustworthy • Sense of humour • Empathy • Patience • Perseverance • Commitment • Cooperative spirit • Strong personal presence • Politically astute/savvy

Source: ARACY, 2013c

This is a very diverse and comprehensive list with many individual competencies such as leadership skills, change management skills and strategic planning, in themselves needing to be unpicked, further developed and contextualised within a collaboration framework. The factsheet does accept that the competencies are extensive and take time to develop. It argues that 'the skills and characteristics of collaboration are different from the norm' and while they are inherent in some people, they can be learnt. But somewhat contradicting its earlier view it states that, some 'everyday' hierarchical skills are transferable to collaborative work, especially those involved in the implementation stages of the policy process.

The work of Emerson and Smutko (2011) distills collaborative competencies from nine different published sources, including US government position descriptions, government documents, practices recommended by the International City/County Management Association, blue ribbon committees and interviews. These competencies are also informed by the authors' extensive experience as facilitators and mediators of public disputes. They refer to competencies as a broader term for mastery of associated knowledge, behaviours and skills. 'Skill sets' in their article refer to a combination of skills, techniques, tools and information that constitute a given competency. Their resulting framework is set out in Table 7.2 and consists of five collaborative competencies encompassing ten specific skill sets that together constitute what the author's term 'collaborative competence'.

In a similar vein, the Office for Personnel Management (2012) offers a competency framework for the Senior Executive Service that includes a core competency on building coalitions as indicated in Table 7.3.

These two frameworks clearly illustrate the different constructions used to interpret competency, although there is some resonance between the constituent elements that are included. O'Leary et al (2012) have also used the notion of a skill set to answer their research question – what is the skill set of the collaborator – which they explored with senior executives in the US government service. Respondents ranked skills into five broad sets – individual attributes (for example, open mindedness, patience, self-confidence, risk-orientation); interpersonal skills (for example, communication, listening); group process skills (for example, facilitation, negotiation, problem-solving, conflict resolution); strategic leadership (for example, visioning, facilitation, creativity); and substantive/technical knowledge. The authors argue that

Table 7.2: A framework for collaborative competence

Competency	Skill set
Leadership and management	• Strengthen collaborative leadership styles and skills • Planning, organising and managing for collaboration, such as collaborative problem-solving and conflict resolution management
Process	• Communicating effectively, including cross-cultural presentations and persuasion • Working in teams and facilitating group decision making • Managing conflict constructively in groups, and from the vantage point of different roles in a group
Analytical	• Applying analytical skills and strategic thinking by understanding political, legal and regulatory contexts • Developing measures of progress and assessing and evaluating performance of the group
Knowledge management	• Integrating technical and scientific information for informed decision making • Using information technology to communicate and operate in social networks
Professional accountability	• Acting on principles of fairness, transparency and inclusiveness • Balancing personal, professional and institutional loyalties with the group's requirements for success

Source: Adapted from Emerson and Smutko, 2011

Table 7.3: Executive core competency: building coalitions competency

Competency	Skill set
Partnering	• Develops networks and build alliances • Collaborates across boundaries to build strategic relationships and achieve common goals
Political savvy	• Identifies the internal and external politics that impact the work of the organisation • Perceives organisational and political reality and acts accordingly
Influencing/negotiating	• Persuades others • Builds consensus through give and take • Gains cooperation from others to obtain information and achieve goals

Source: Adapted from Office for Public Management, 2012

the findings particularly emphasise relational attributes and endorse Salaman's (2002) observation that they represent: 'a shift in emphasis from management skills and control of large bureaucratic organisations to enablement skills – the skills required to engage partners that are arrayed horizontally in networks and to bring multiple stakeholders together for a common end in a situation of interdependence'.

Other frameworks that purport to reflect the requirements for managing in collaboration use different methodologies. The following two are worthy of note – one based on qualities and the other on capabilities. First, the government of South Australia has adopted a 'joined-up' approach to the design and delivery of its services (Government of South Australia, 2016c). Its approach involves a combination of both structural elements and mechanisms to support and increase the competency of managers to undertake effective collaboration. The strategy was partly informed by feedback from existing middle managers on their experiences of collaboration. These included views and opinions that pointed to the biggest barriers to collaboration being a lack of shared vision, priorities and common purpose; managers working in silos, not knowing who does what and who to collaborate with; a culture favouring the status quo over collaboration and innovation; and a lack of permission or support from top management to collaborate. Conversely, middle managers considered the most important factors supporting collaboration to be high level leadership; support for champions; clear, shared outcomes, focused vision and accountability; appropriate skills, trust and respect between internal and external collaborators; and having networks and contacts in other agencies. The delivery report (Government of South Australia, 2016c) takes the view that:

> collaborative and joined-up approaches require a particular skill set that is often lacking or poorly developed in many staff. This can result in people retreating back to the 'silos' approach. However, there are few clear examples of systematic up-skilling. To be effective and sustainable there needs to be investment in training to enable the development of these skills.

In addition, the report proposes that certain managers need to be identified as: 'champion leaders or change agents...who can nurture the right skills and attitudes among staff, undertake creative problem solving, craft "workarounds" and harness collaborative opportunities. This "craftsmanship" often requires people to stretch outside of formal structures or boundaries in order to facilitate collaborative working.' These managers, also referred to as 'intrapreneurs', are considered to be pivotal in delivering effective collaboration and need 'sufficient autonomy, freedom and flexibility to get the work done, and trust from senior levels in the champion's ability to carry out the work to meet agency and government policy goals'. The issue that is not altogether clear is the extent to which these 'new responsibilities' are included in current job descriptions or whether they need to be substantially re-written. However, the qualities sought of such people are those detailed in Table 7.4.

Interestingly, this mixture of qualities resonates well with the three themes considered to be central to the management of collaboration in this book – particularly the focus on relationship building, understanding complexity through a systems approach and the need to forge common purpose.

Bingham et al (2008: 274) use the notion of 'capability' when setting out their view of what public managers need to have when operating in collaboration emphasising 'the sense of being able to do, not simply being passively competent'. These capabilities are:

- designing a network with the necessary players at the table: this centres on knowing when to collaborate and with whom, and the different motivations and interests of multiple stakeholders;
- structuring governance for the collaborative group: this is particularly crucial for any successful collaboration – designing decision-making processes, rules of engagement, communication systems, accountability frameworks and ways of working – creating the collaborative culture;
- negotiating ethically to best leverage agency resources: given the diverse range of interests and views in collaborative settings, negotiation skills are arguably foremost in the skill

Table 7.4: Qualities sought in joined-up champions/change agents

Quality	Description
Good negotiator	To prioritise the core requirements for their agency and determine what elements can be negotiated. They will be able to assess the needs and requirements of other agencies and then enter into discussions with a good understanding of how they are going to manage conversations and reach agreement on mutually agreed priorities.
Excellent listener	Spends more time actively listening to their stakeholders than speaking. They know that understanding other positions is critical to success.
Good facilitator	Will help groups find out where participants in the process agree and don't agree and find agreed solutions.
Innovator	Will value innovation, and is prepared to try new things and take risks. They may be less conventional in their approach. They will question the status quo, be observant, experiment and network
Intrapreneurs	Will exercise initiative and pursue opportunities. An intrapreneur is able to strategically assess the political environment and work out the best way to take advantage of the opportunities as they present themselves.
Excellent communicator	Someone with strong verbal and written communication skills.
Strong relationship builder	Demonstrates the importance of building and maintaining relationships with others in their team
Systems thinker	Takes a holistic approach on the way a system's constituent parts interrelate and how systems work over time and within the context of larger systems.
Respectfulness	Valuing diversity and recognising the importance of drawing on a broad range of skills.
Ability to compromise	Knowing there is no point being rigid in collaborative processes.
Strong political acumen	Demonstrating a high consciousness of internal politics and the political environment in which the government operates.

Source: Government of South Australia, 2016c

set of effective collaborative managers – these embrace active listening and communication, suspending judgement, transparency, empathy and demonstrating creativity to devise solutions that transcend individual interests;

- facilitating meetings of the network: again this is a key capability that aims to secure the involvement and contribution of all parties in a constructive manner;
- managing conflict among network members: conflict is inevitable, so conflict management skills are necessary to ensure equal and fair participation of members;
- effectively engaging the public: collaborative approaches to policy design and delivery can often be confusing to citizens and communities because of their inherent complexities around accountability and who does what. Therefore, designing effective public engagement strategies for collaboration needs to be an integral part of a manager's armory;
- designing useful systems for evaluating the outcomes of collaboration: typically the 'Cinderella' of the policymaking process, evaluation is a crucial element that needs particular tools, models, frameworks and approaches;
- operating within the legal constraints on collaborative public agency action: 'understanding the scope of existing legal infrastructure as it provides authority and incentives, or presents constraints, obstacles, and barriers, is an important form of explicit knowledge that can shape practice' (p. 280).

Finally, a flavour of the competencies indicated above is repeated by expert practitioners and agency officials in their observations of leaders of interagency groups interviewed in a GAO Report (2014: 27) – the following five competencies identified were: 'worked well with people, communicated openly with a range of stakeholders, built and maintained relationships, understood other points of view, and set a vision for the group'. The thrust of the evidence presented so far echoes with the findings of this book in relation to the essence of collaborative management by middle managers – managing for common purpose, managing complexity and interdependencies and managing relationships. Figure 7.2 details the competencies that are needed to put these into practice – in various permutations and combinations depending on the particular challenges faced.

Figure 7.2: Collaborative competencies for middle managers

Managing for commmon purpose Managing complexity and interdependencies Managing relationships		
Multi-lensed and strategic Consensus-seeking and teamwork Negotation and diplomacy	Facilitative and enabling leadership Analytical skills Networking and communication	Building and sustaining trust Collaborative knowledge Professional and moral value base

Education, training and development

In the light of this discussion of the desired profiles of middle managers working in collaboration, the focus now turns to the implications of this for education, training, learning and development. Bingham et al (2008: 281) argue that: 'in public management, we must align our pedagogy with the realities that public management occurs in networks of many different actors'. This suggests a fundamental shift in the status quo that arguably has yet to fully embrace this radical change across public services in many countries. For instance, a graduate development programme sponsored by the Local Government Association in England is based on a course content that includes financial management, procurement and commissioning, project and people management, community engagement and how to work in a political context, but nothing on managing in collaboration. Degree and other accredited programmes in public management, professional development programmes and management development programmes need to better reflect the competencies and capabilities required to manage in collaboration. The implications affect what theoretical and empirical knowledge is required, and what skills, abilities and behaviours are necessary for effective collaborative practice.

The nature of formal education

The education sector and formal programmes of study lead to various levels of attainment reflected in certificates and degrees. These can be of assorted durations – part or full time, undergraduate or postgraduate – and delivered at the formative stages of a student's career or at a more mature age. Business Studies Programmes and MBAs are typical routes for aspiring and experienced managers, although these are overwhelmingly contextualised in a private sector context. Typical course structures for undergraduate programmes focus on finance and accounting; managing people; marketing; strategy; law; organisational behaviour; entrepreneurship; and business analysis and quantitative methods. At a Masters level in Management or Business Administration, these core modules are generally repeated with the addition of subjects such as leadership, decision-making processes, ethics and corporate social responsibility, and modules that are geared to particular career paths. In addition, many of these courses are internationalised to reflect trends in globalisation and multinational operations. A number of more leading-edge academic institutions, as well as offering the usual recipe including managing people, finance, marketing and strategy, include modules that examine more about the behaviour and governance of organisations through politics, power, culture, working in teams, managing change and organisational performance, complexity and working in networks – themes that have more relevance to working in collaboration rather than working within organisations.

A comparatively more recent growth of programmes at a postgraduate and Masters level has specifically been designed for students seeking careers in Public Administration and Management. Some of these are generic and designed to appeal to students in government, government agencies and third sector organisations, and others are tailored to specific policy areas such as healthcare or environmental science. Masters degree courses in Public Administration (MPA) have core modules on the policymaking process, governance, leadership, public administration, organisational change and politics – all contextualised within the public sector and the provision of public services. There are examples of MPA programmes that reflect collaborative working much more than others. For instance, the University of Melbourne MPA is marketed as being able to deliver learning outcomes that include:

- a comprehensive understanding and appreciation of the interconnectedness and complexity of the fields of public management and administration, and of the key public management practices required to most effectively deliver outcomes;
- well-developed interpersonal and communication skills necessary to a range of managerial and administrative activities including report writing, workplace discussions, negotiation and management and lobbying strategies;
- the ability to draw upon an extensive repertoire of advanced managerial and administrative skills including skills in leadership, negotiation, decision analysis and strategic management;
- the ability to draw upon an extensive repertoire of advanced professional skills, in particular in decision-making, providing advice and collaborating across sectors.

The focus of this programme certainly resonates much more with the needs of managing in collaboration outlined in previous chapters, and more mainstreamed into the course structure rather than being treated as a bolt-on elective module as is the case with others. However, such programmes are generally in the minority across the globe – a rather perverse situation given the vast number of managers who are employed in government, government agencies and the public sector in general.

An additional issue that is somewhat out of the scope of this book concerns not only the content and structure of courses, but how they are taught and delivered. Much of what the thrust of this book has discussed concerns managing in a particular form of governance – about building relationships, political skills, listening and communicating, negotiating around common purpose and making sense of complex policy interrelationships. The challenge for learning is to strike the right balance between the teaching of explicit knowledge about collaboration in the form of facts, theories, models and approaches, with the development of tacit knowledge and experiential learning that assists in practical policymaking and practice. The cultivation of reflective practice in middle managers through the use of case studies, videos, study visits and other mechanisms will improve the capacities of students to manage in collaborative arenas. Another important decision revolves around whether mainstream public management modules and indeed, some business studies modules, should offer dedicated modules on collaborative management, or whether it should be weaved into other relevant modules. Perhaps a combination of both approaches would be preferable?

Inter-professional learning in collaboration

A large proportion of middle managers working in the public sector have careers that evidence strong professional backgrounds and identities. Their management experience and career progression has been a result of the acquisition of a core body of professional knowledge, and scaling the organisational hierarchy within that defined professional area. Any knowledge of management – either related to within organisations or collaboratively – would have been acquired through the relevant professional education. It might be argued that some professional training is more relevant than others in preparing them for working in collaboration. A number of middle managers with a social work background interviewed in my research argued that they were better prepared for the challenges involved in working with actors from other organisations because of their well-developed communication and relationship skills. These contrasted with professionals in technical and scientific disciplines who were cocooned within positivist paradigms that placed a high value on 'facts' and certainty. The general question then of whether some professions are more geared, or better equipped to work in collaboration, needs to be explored further.

This suggests that the strength of professional ties can be both an advantage and disadvantage when working in collaborative settings – a strength because of the expertise and knowledge that it brings in a particular policy area or topic, but potentially a disadvantage when it comes to compromising and sharing power, and expressing a willingness to take other so-called 'non-professional' views into account. The feedback from numerous studies of collaboration highlighted the irritation that many participants felt about actors who were unprepared to compromise and constantly reinforced, or hid behind, their professional area of expertise – jealously guarding it and setting up 'Berlin Walls' to ward off potential incursions into their territory.

As a consequence of this, there is a clear challenge for ongoing inter-professional learning in collaborative situations, but also one that might have implications for core professional education. One research study (Gallagher, 2008) that focused on multi-agency working across health, mental health, social services and criminal justice in Northern Ireland, refers to collaboration as 'co-configuration' where there is 'interdependency between multiple producers in a strategic alliance or other pattern of partnership which collaboratively creates and maintains a complex package which integrates products and services and has a long life cycle' (Gallagher, 2008: 23). It argues that in co-configuration 'there is a need to go beyond conventional team work or networking, to the practice of knotworking, a rapidly changing, distributed and partially improvised orchestration of collaborative performance which takes place between otherwise loosely connected actors and their work systems to support clients' and 'expertise in such contexts is best understood as the collaborative and discursive construction of tasks, solutions, visions, breakdowns and innovations. It requires participants to have a disposition to recognise and engage with the expertise distributed across rapidly shifting professional groupings'. The consequences of this interpretation of collaboration for learning are twofold – first, learning for co-configuration is about renegotiation and re-imagining of collaborative relations and practices, and their conversion into new systems and practices, and second, learning in co-configuration where actors and their organisations learn from interactions with users. The specific conclusions of the research study were that a number of interpersonal and organisational practices needed to be put in place as follows:

• Personal relationships based on trust are fundamental, both to secure tangible rather than aspirational outcomes, and to offer symbolic leadership to actors in collaborative agencies that are not necessarily involved in collaborative work.

• There is a need to rapidly capture and codify emergent collaborative practice into formal systems and policies.

• There is a need to recognise and preserve the different identities of professionals and their organisations when operating in collaboration, and there must be clear benefits for all participants.

This latter point underscores a view that interagency work does not necessarily erode boundaries but can result in them being reinforced. Warmington et al (2004) argue that:

> some practitioners working in interagency settings may reinforce professional divisions by, for instance, appealing to the client's interests. Some may use professional boundaries to identify lines of accountability and responsibility. Paradoxically, managerial attempts to develop 'organic, generic, overlapped, non-hierarchical ways of working' may drive boundaries into the 'subjective territory of the worker's own intuitive framework of what constitutes nursing or social work – where they will be relatively immune to change'. In short, where boundaries are not codified organizationally they may be re-inscribed subjectively and intuitively.

They proceed to argue that: 'standard notions of professional expertise imply a vertical model, in which practitioners develop in competence over time as they acquire new levels of professional knowledge, graduating 'upwards' level by level in their own specialism. By contrast, boundary-crossing suggests that expertise is also developed when practitioners collaborate *horizontally* across sectors.' Also, 'whereas standard professional role theories tend to focus on anxieties over professional barriers… notions of boundary crossing suggest that new developments in learning for interagency working should focus upon the potential spaces for renegotiation of professional practice that are opened up when workers from traditionally separate sectors begin collaborating' (Warmington et al, 2004). The notion of boundary-crossing enables collaboration to be conceived of in terms of the spaces created for renegotiation of professional practices and reconfiguration of professional identities; implying a creative movement between traditionally separate professional cultures, perceptions and practices, and encompassing internal tensions as well as consensus. Whether this results in improved inter-professional working or the emergence of new types of professional is an interesting question.

The evidence of a Cochrane Review (Reeves et al, 2018) into strategies to improve interprofessional collaboration in health and social care is underwhelming. It concluded that: 'strategies to improve interprofessional collaboration between health and social care professionals may slightly improve patient functional status, professionals' adherence to recommended practices, and the use of healthcare resources' and 'due to the lack of clear evidence, we are uncertain whether the strategies improved patient-assessed quality of care, continuity of care, or collaborative working'.

Inter-professional competency frameworks

A number of competency frameworks have been developed in an effort to reflect and promote inter-professional collaboration particularly in education and training. The notion of interprofessionality has been defined as:

> the process by which professionals reflect on and develop ways of practicing that provides an integrated and cohesive answer to the needs of the client/family/ population...[I]t involves continuous interaction and knowledge sharing between professionals, organised to solve or explore a variety of education and care issues all while seeking to optimise the patient's participation...Interprofessionality requires a paradigm shift, since interprofessional practice has unique characteristics in terms of values, codes of conduct, and ways of working. These characteristics must be elucidated. (D'Amour and Oandasan, 2005: 9)

The manner in which these characteristics are elucidated is through the development of competency frameworks. These exist in a number of countries particularly in the fields of health and social care. One such example in Canada (CIHC, 2010: 8) defines interprofessional collaboration as 'the process of developing and maintaining effective interprofessional working relationships with learners, practitioners, patients/clients/families and communities to enable optimal health outcomes'. A framework is developed based on six competency domains that highlight the knowledge, skills, attitudes and values that shape the judgements essential for interprofessional collaborative practice – four central domains including: role clarification, team functioning, addressing interprofessional conflict and collaborative leadership; and two domains that support the others related to: interprofessional communication and patient/client/family/community-centred care. The framework suggests that the complexity of the situation, the context of practice and the need for quality improvement influence the way in which the framework is applied; and it is developmental and flexible in nature to reflect the dynamic and changing nature of practice and individual's learning potential.

In a similar vein, IPEC (2016) has constructed a framework setting out the core competencies for interprofessional collaborative practice in US healthcare professions. Its purpose is to 'broaden the scope and increase the momentum of the transformation of interprofessional education of health professionals' (IPEC, 2016: 3). The framework itself comprises Interprofessional Collaboration as a central domain consisting of four core general competencies and related sub-competencies. The four competencies are:

1. Values/Ethics for Interprofessional Practice: to build up a climate of mutual respect and shared values;
2. Roles/Responsibilities: to use the knowledge of one's own role and those of other professionals appropriately to address healthcare needs;
3. Interprofessional Communication: to communicate widely with fellow professionals and users;
4. Teams and Teamwork: to apply relationship-building values and the principles of team dynamics to performing

effectively in different roles to plan, deliver and evaluate healthcare.

The report of an Expert Panel on Interprofessional Collaborative Practice (IEPC, 2011: 7) considers that core competencies are needed in order to:

- create a coordinated effort across the health professions to embed essential content in all health professions education curricula;
- guide professional and institutional curricular development of learning approaches and assessment strategies to achieve productive outcomes;
- provide the foundation for a learning continuum in interprofessional competency development across the professions and the lifelong learning trajectory;
- prompt dialogue to evaluate the 'fit' between educationally identified core competencies for interprofessional collaborative practice and practice needs/demands;
- find opportunities to integrate essential interprofessional education content consistent with current accreditation expectations for each health profession's education programme.

A WHO Report (2010) sets out a policy framework for action on interprofessional education to secure collaborative practices among health professionals. The framework recommends a number of mechanisms to shape interprofessional education divided into those relating to the educators and those to the curricula. Similarly, mechanisms that are considered to be influential in shaping collaborative practices are listed as those relating to institutional support, working cultures and environmental factors.

Middle management development programmes

The reality for many middle managers operating in collaborative arenas is that their knowledge and practice in this form of governance will be developed through experience supplemented by ad hoc development and training opportunities and programmes. These might be one-off events involving a particular topic or skill, delivered in-house or through a commissioned academic or consultancy provider; they might involve a programme of training specifically provided for the members of a particular collaborative group; or they might involve a more intensive opportunity to learn about collaborative management.

Job rotations

One such mechanism for improving the appropriateness and effectiveness of collaborative management is through various forms of inter-organisational secondment and job rotation. A National Academy of Public Administration Report (2007: 211) asserted that: 'in this day and age, cross-cutting, boundary-spanning problems are the norm; as a consequence, the case for interagency mobility assignments as a way of developing SES candidates for a whole-of-government role is even more compelling than it was in 1979' and 'this demands leaders who are able to see the big picture, take an enterprise point of view, employ certain *enterprise* leadership competencies to overcome agency-centric stovepipes – and achieve...interagency unity of effort...and that mobility is the only effective way to develop those competencies'. In the context of US National security, a study involving mid to senior level employees participating in a one- to three-year rotation programme set out a number of benefits for the participants and their host and home agencies (Box 7.3).

Box 7.3: Benefits of job rotation scheme

- Effective interagency rotations help achieve collaboration-related results by improving the participant's knowledge of other agencies, building the participant's leadership and collaboration skills and experience, and offering the participant opportunities to form interagency networks.
- The participant's home agency can increase its capacity to collaborate by leveraging the participant's experience.

- The home agency can ensure that it has an adequate supply of current and future leaders with the broad perspectives, collaboration skills and other competencies necessary to succeed in an interagency environment.
- The participant's host agency can benefit from the temporary increase in workforce capacity, as well as from applying the participant's particular skills, experiences, or other characteristics to a specific mission or project.
- The host agency can build its network with the home agency, using its relationship with the participant for future collaboration once he or she has returned to the home agency.

Source: GAO, 2012b: 6

Secondment and rotation programmes can, however, sometimes be rather tokenistic and unplanned, resulting in a failure to achieve the outcomes expected. A number of barriers, both for the host and home organisation, have to be addressed to realise the full potential of such initiatives. What is also important is that such programmes need to be part of a wider set of initiatives designed to improve collaboration, such as, organisational structures and culture, planning processes and funding, not just those relating to workforce capabilities, and rotation programmes need to support the particular aims and goals of collaboration between agencies.

The GAO Report (2012b) identified a number of specific incentives to encourage participation in rotation programmes, including tapping into potential participants' internal motivations relating to the role of collaboration; using performance management systems to recognise and reward performance outside the home agency (for example, collaboration-related competency); factoring in rotations to promotion decisions; and publicly recognising rotation performance with award schemes. In addition, participating agencies can support rotation programmes through high level leadership endorsing such initiatives; gaining agreement on interagency governance mechanism relating to roles, responsibilities, relocation costs, salaries and accountability arrangements; rewarding managers for supporting such programmes; focusing on high level performing participants; ensuring a careful match between participants and new roles; supporting their training and developing needs; and making the best use of returning participants because 'if the knowledge, skills, and networks gained through an interagency rotation are not used in the short-term, they can be lost or become irrelevant' (GAO, 2012b: 13).

Communities of practice

Snyder and de Souza Briggs (2003: 4) argue that because contemporary public problems and challenges are highly complex, there needs to be: 'a commensurate capacity for learning, innovation, and collaboration across diverse constituencies' but 'existing models of teamwork and collaboration, while useful, are hard-pressed to overcome persistent barriers: bureaucratic inertia, fear of change, and turf-minded managers, among others. And many change efforts are much too dependent on charismatic champions whose exits spell the demise of promising innovation'. They further comment that:

> conventional government bureaucracies – designed to solve stable problems for established constituencies through centrally managed programs and policies – are hampered by important limitations in this environment. While scale and functional specialization still offer important benefits, and while centralized coordination and enforcement of standards also have a role to play, the old structures are not enough.

The value of networking has constantly been stressed by actors involved in collaborative working, both as a source of intelligence, and more particularly, as a means of building and sustaining relationships with people whom they are likely to partner. The nature and extent of these networks are largely a matter for each individual, but they can be supported and enhanced through communities of practice – a type of collaborative action-learning network that combine various interests, professions, sectors and capabilities across boundaries. Communities of practice are more familiar within specific professional groupings, and collaborative or cross-sector communities are much less common.

Box 7.4: What is a collaborative community of practice?

- Communities of practice are a particularly appropriate structural model for cross-agency and cross-sector collaborations because they are inherently boundary-crossing entities.
- They operate as 'social learning systems' where practitioners connect to solve problems, share ideas, set standards, build tools and develop relationships with peers and stakeholders.
- An essential dimension of a community of practice is voluntary participation, because without this a member is less likely to seek or share knowledge; build trust and reciprocity with others; or apply the community's knowledge in practice.
- Communities of practice complement the function of formal units, such as departments or cross-functional teams, whose primary purpose is to deliver a product or service and to assume accountability for quality, cost and customer satisfaction. A salient benefit of communities, in fact, is to bridge formal organisational boundaries in order to increase the collective knowledge, skills and professional trust and reciprocity of practitioners who serve in these organisations.
- Communities of practice are effective mechanisms for building and disseminating capabilities because they address the 'local' nature of knowledge – as well as issues related to skill and will.
- Communities of practice provide a living repository for ideas, information, best practices, directories of experts and resources.
- Communities of practice are effective for integrating new dimensions into established capabilities.
- Communities of practice build organisational capabilities by providing professionals with a forum for learning; for testing ideas and innovations; and for building relationships and a sense of professional identity with colleagues.
- A community of practice comprises three structural dimensions: its domain, community and practice. The domain refers to its focus and identity; the community to its member relationships and interactions,

and the practice to its methods and learning initiatives including both best practices and tacit skills.

Source: Snyder and de Souza Briggs (2003)

Communities of Practice (CoPs) have been described as:

> self-organising and self-governing groups of people who share a passion for the domain of what they do and strive to be better practitioners. They pursue a shared learning agenda and they create value for their members and stakeholders through developing and spreading new knowledge, practices, capabilities and organisational capacity. They create knowledge networks across professional and hierarchical boundaries, and access the intelligence that is everywhere in the system. CoPs have become intentional strategies for boundary-crossing, integrative and rigorous sharing of practice. (Health Innovation Network, 2015)

An excellent Communities of Practice Resource Kit (Center for State, Tribal and Territorial Support, 2012) developed for public health but with much wider applicability considers that CoPs have three elements – community that enables interaction through discussions, collaborative activities and relationship building; shared domain of interest; and shared practice of experiences, stories, tools and ways of addressing recurring problems. This guide contains detailed advice relating to the design, launching, sustaining, evolution and evaluation of CoPs. Important features of CoPs are that: 'rather than operating in silos, the CoPs work across programs, disciplines, organizations, and geographic regions to identify and address issues of broad applicability' and they 'are fundamentally informal, or at least less formally organised than the teams, advisory boards, or work groups that are often used in public health' (Mabery et al, 2013: 234).

Setting aside problems of organisation, resourcing and servicing, they can perform a valuable role in helping to build social capital at a local geographical or policy level, and such networks can offer a home for some actors who might feel isolated within their own organisations and seek the support of others in similar situations. Seminars, workshops, study visits, websites, teleconferencing, joint projects and joint training sessions are all potentially useful activities of a collaborative community of practice. The product of such activities lies not just in the exchange of 'explicit' areas of knowledge, but also in encouraging the transfer of 'tacit' knowledge between different professionals, and as a means of shining a light on the worldviews and assumptions of different actors in an informal, 'safe space' – that is outside the formal working structures of employing organisations. New technology and social media offer effective mechanisms for maintaining communication between members including, 'creating networking profiles to help build relationships, online discussions to facilitate learning, idea banks to share knowledge, and web conferencing to promote action' (Canadian Health Services Research Foundation, 2007: 1). Mabery et al (2013: 234) concluded that: 'the CoP model is not only a vehicle for deepening knowledge and expertise among members and solving common public health problems, but is also a strategy for enhancing relationships and bi-directional knowledge transfer'; that the results of an evaluation study proved that: 'a well-facilitated, member-driven, and highly participative CoP can build needed social capital, thereby bridging organisational silos to develop and enrich professional networks for sharing, learning, and collaborating'; and 'the results reveal clear benefits to individual members, their organisations, and public health disciplines including daily work efficiencies, expanded infrastructure, and enhanced relationships between Centres of Disease Control and Prevention and its public health partners' (p. 226). Drawing on the work of Wenger (1998), Mabery et al (2013) produce a summary of the benefits of communities of practice captured in Table 7.5. In addition to individual and organisational benefits, there are those that are realised at a domain level and vary according to the particular policy/issues concerned, but are likely to include, increased communication, enhanced analytical and domain-specific capabilities, and better links between dispersed practitioners, as well as contributing

Table 7.5: Benefits of communities of practice

	Benefits
Individuals	• Continual learning and professional development • Access to expertise • Improved communication with peers • Increased productivity and quality of work • Networking for staying current in the field • Sense of professional identity • Enhanced professional reputation
Organisations	• Faster, less costly retrieval of information and reduced learning curves • Knowledge sharing and distribution • Coordination, standardisation and synergy across organisational units • Reduced rework and reinvention • Innovation • Benchmarking against and influencing industry standards • Alliance building

Source: Adapted from Mabery et al, 2013

to overall government efficiency and effectiveness, and the promotion of consistent quality and standards.

Snyder and de Souza Briggs (2003: 50) make an important point about the role of collaborative communities of practice in relation to the formal structures of government. They suggest that: 'they complement formal institutions by crossing boundaries and fostering learning and innovation. They contribute to a cross-hatching structure that combines a focus on service delivery with the capacity to cross boundaries to discover and diffuse innovations'. In such a system:

> formal political and service delivery organisations are still held accountable for using resources to get results related to social outcomes – they are *resource management structures*. In this role, they set strategic direction and policies, manage conflicts, and embody public values. Meanwhile, the communities of practice are responsible for building and sharing information, ideas, skills, methods, and influence to enable organisations to get things done – they are *capacity-building structures*.

Capacity building programmes

Capacity building programmes are another means of increasing the effectiveness of individuals and groups engaged in collaborative working. The independence of external facilitation is often a helpful catalyst in promoting openness between participants, and certainly joint training and development events provide the opportunity for shared learning and knowledge exchange. The use of so-called 'Partnership Health Checks' is a useful method of assessing and monitoring the dynamics of collaborative groups, and for the identification of any training or development needs. Capacity building programmes can be relevant at different levels of governance – at a local level focused on individual collaborations, but also at a regional or national level aiming to raise collaborative capacities over a much wider system and sometimes associated with major structural re-organisations or the introduction of new financial frameworks or statutory duties. The Government of South Australia's initiative previously discussed is an example of this approach.

Similarly, an IBM Center for the Business of Government Report (Barclay, 2013) referring to the US government points to the need to nurture and train a specific cadre of senior executives to work on managing and leading cross-agency initiatives. It argues that while many have the necessary skills and competencies to do the job, 'the opportunities, incentives and support systems' are not in place to promote mobility across sectors. Typical barriers include that: 'home agencies are narrowly focused on their own programme performance and protecting their own resources', 'collaboration is difficult at best and runs against prevailing incentives and agency value systems', and 'performance management focuses largely on single-agency, rather than interagency and broad network outcomes' (Barclay, 2013: 7). To counter this situation, the Report proposes to create a pool or cadre of senior executives to work as cross-agency executives, and to serve as catalysts for cross-agency initiatives. These executives would ideally have inter-sectoral experience, and development competencies in six main areas of competence – strategic management and thinking skills; shared leadership and people skills; performance management capability; joint management; business management; and management technology savvy and proficiency. In addition, it recommends that such an initiative should be coordinated centrally at a government-wide level, or perhaps, local governance level. While this proposal is largely pitched at a senior executive and leadership level, the merits of such scheme are worthy of exploration at a middle management level. However, there are many hurdles to overcome in relation to contracts of employment, remuneration and other HRM issues, plus there is the danger of perpetuating a view that collaboration is the job of a specialised group of actors rather than one that needs to be mainstreamed into the roles of a wider set of public managers.

Incentives and rewards for collaborative working

One very important issue that needs to be clarified concerns the mechanisms used to motivate, incentivise and reward public managers working in collaboration. If they are not suitable, it is likely that they will present a significant barrier to collaborative working particularly to those that are somewhat reluctant to wholeheartedly embrace this form of management. Important questions to resolve include: 'Is it appropriate to modify existing staff appraisal systems and performance-pay regimes and adapt or extend them to collaborative working?' and 'Can you relate performance-based pay to collaborative working especially in situations where control is not dependent upon the actions of single managers, but upon a collection of managers from different organisations?' Ingraham and Getha-Taylor are firmly of the belief that 'individually-based performance systems can threaten the very fabric of collaboration' (1998: 88), and that the problem of pay-for-performance is that its focus is on the past and present and neglects the developmental effort that is required to build collaborative capital and relationships. The discussion needs to consider basic issues concerning the motivation of public managers and whether it is connected to financial reward, self-worth, a public service ethos, the ability to influence situations or a mix of all of these. Working in collaboration invariably offers public managers the prospect of increased recognition outside the normal course of their duties, and potentially very interesting work. Ingraham and Getha-Taylor argue that 'rewarding collaboration requires a new set of assumptions including the acknowledgement that collaboration is not an individual endeavour, that collaborative performance is driven by many factors (the least of which may be finance), and that many indispensable collaborative skills cannot be easily measured' (1998: 94).

An ARACY factsheet (2013c) suggests that collaboration between actors working in cross-boundary situations would be enhanced by a number of supportive human resource management practices including, establishing flexible recruitment and hiring processes; changing organisational norms and culture to support collaboration, in particular gearing reward systems toward collaboration; including the requirement for collaborative behaviour in job descriptions, setting goals related to cross-boundary work, and acknowledging those who exhibit collaborative behaviours; introducing arrangements that facilitate the work of the collaboration – for example, open access to funding and resource supports; and developing accountability and reporting regimes that reflect shared effort and responsibility, including performance indicators for collaborative behaviour and actions, the formation of shared revenue streams and establishing agreed reporting criteria. These are far from straightforward to design and enact because HRM are primarily focused within the structure and operations of single agencies. This issue does raise the very important question of the extent to which the structure, organisation and culture of a particular agency makes it more or less able to work in collaborative forms of practice.

Key points of learning

- A number of **frameworks** have been developed that set out the competencies that are needed by middle managers to be effective in managing in collaboration. They differ in their interpretation of the notion of competency and variously refer to skills, behaviours, capabilities, qualities, personality traits and knowledge.

- The findings on the **skills and competencies** needed by middle managers to work in collaboration have implications on the design and delivery of formal education and academic programmes at all levels of study. A key question revolves around whether mainstream public management modules and business studies modules, should offer dedicated modules on collaborative management, or whether it should be weaved into other relevant modules.

- Working in collaboration presents a challenge to the nature of inter-professional learning, and different views are advanced on the merits of aiming to preserve or blur boundaries. A number of **competency frameworks** have been developed to promote inter-professional collaboration in education and training. These emphasise communication, working in teams, shared value systems, conflict management and role clarification.

- A range of middle management development programmes and practices can be used to support managing in collaboration. These include **secondment, mentoring**, CoPs and capacity building programmes.

- Effective **inter-agency rotations** can help by improving knowledge of other agencies, building leadership and collaboration skills and experience, and offering opportunities to form interagency networks. There are benefits for the home agency through an increase in its collaborative capacity and experience, and for the host agency in terms of a temporary increase in workforce capacity, as well as the particular skills and experiences of the secondee. Experience suggests that such programmes need to be carefully planned to avoid tokenism and ineffectiveness.

- **Collaborative Communities of Practice** are a valuable mechanism for supporting collaborative working in dispersed policy/geographical areas involving multiple and diverse actors. Their benefits can be realised at the levels of the individual, organisation and domain and include, shared learning, peer group support, increased communication, stimulation of innovation and networking. Effective CoPs do require a sustained investment in leadership, design and organisation and need to be evaluated on a regular basis.

• There are a number of **supportive HRM practices** that need to be developed to support collaborative working including, establishing flexible recruitment and hiring processes; changing organisational norms and culture to support collaboration, setting goals related to cross-boundary work, and developing accountability and reporting regimes that reflect shared responsibility.

• In particular, **mechanisms to motivate, incentivise and reward** middle managers working in collaboration need to be developed. Staff appraisal systems and performance pay-regimes need to embrace or be adapted for collaborative working.

Suggested further reading

ARACY (2013) *Collaborative Competencies/Capabilities (Factsheet 14)*, Canberra: ARACY

Center for State, Tribal and Territorial Support (2012) *Communities of Practice Resource Kit*, Atlanta, GA: US Department of Health and Human Services

Getha-Taylor, H. (2008) 'Identifying collaborative competencies', *Review of Public Personnel Administration*, Vol. 28 (2), pp. 103–119

Snyder, W.M. and de Souza Briggs, X. (2003) *Communities of Practice: A New Tool for Government Managers*, Arlington, VA: IBM Centre for the Business of Government

8

Reflections and conclusion

> Many of government's most important programs require effective horizontal communication and management, yet too much of government still operates within vertical silos that hinder horizontal collaboration. The government increasingly suffers from what we call an advanced case of bureausclerosis, caused by increasing administrative layers and walls between policymakers and the administrators charged with carrying out policy. (National Academy of Public Administration, 2017: 10)

This final chapter brings the book to a conclusion with a summary of, and reflections on the main themes, arguments and perspectives examined in this book. It aims to place this contribution within the existing literature, as well as setting out a future research agenda on this topic of study in terms of research questions, themes, methodologies and areas of study. This book has explored the implications of the changing face of public management, policy and governance on a particular cadre of public managers – the 'middle managers'. It has not been a straightforward task to clearly demark and categorise this group of actors. The term 'middle' suggests a positional perspective that locates these managers in a particular tier within a traditionally organised bureaucratic organisation – sandwiched between a top tier of executives, and a bottom layer of primarily frontline professionals, administrative, support and clerical staff. However, middle managers can also be categorised by role, nature of work and activities. It has been argued that they represent a potentially influential group of actors who wield power and influence through their position and control over financial resources and staff. Their power is invariably underpinned by a professional grounding in a specific area of knowledge and expertise. Arguably, middle managers comprise the heart of an organisation, but their role is challenged by a myriad of tensions and competing accountabilities. Managing people and budgets, meeting targets and mediating between upward and downward pressures are uncomfortable facts of their working lives – hence, frequent complaints of being a member of the 'squeezed middle class'.

The design and delivery of public services has been driven by different approaches over recent decades – moving from Public Administration to New Public Management and more recently to New Public Governance. However, in practice the differences between these broad approaches are blurred and examples of each of these models are alive and kicking. The discussion in Chapter 2 aims briefly to track the implications of these approaches for the role of middle managers, culminating in a more detailed analysis and exploration of the impact of collaborative forms of governance on this group of public managers. The thrust of the treatise rests on the observation that working in collaboration will continue to strengthen in both depth and breadth across the public policy landscape as a result of the prevalence of highly complex and interdependent issues and problems demanding efficient, effective and responsive policy solutions. These require people and organisations to work collaboratively across multiple boundaries, for example of profession, agency and governance. This must be tempered by a warning not to consider all public problems as 'wicked', and to appreciate that many can be dealt with predominantly by single organisations operating autonomously without the need for collaboration. The danger for public policy makers is to avoid being seduced by constant exhortations to work in collaboration when single agency management is more appropriate. Nevertheless, the implications for middle managers working in this current and emerging policy environment is that their role, competencies and behaviours need to respond accordingly. The discussion in the earlier chapters of the book suggests that middle managers in general have been equipped to work within the confines of their own organisation, but working collaboratively presents a new challenge, and arguably, demands a different approach and skill set. Crucially, middle managers face the challenge of needing to manage in different forms of governance with its attendant tensions, ambiguities and sensitivities.

The literature – both theoretical and empirical – on management and middle managers is extensive, albeit with a private sector bias. However, parallels in collaborative settings, with some notable exceptions, are less developed. Chapter 2 examines the literature on collaborative public management together with the work on 'boundary spanners' (Williams, 2012a), network managers (Child, 2006) and collaborative public managers (Agranoff, 2012). This research details the behaviours, strategies, tactics and roles of the public actors together with the skills, attributes, competencies and personality traits deemed necessary to undertake them. Taking a view that 'leadership' is not the unique responsibility of those few executives at the head of the organisation, but also an important element of a middle manager's domain, an interrogation of the literature on leadership approaches in collaboration offers important insights and perspectives on this subject, highlighting contrasts with traditionally orientated intra-organisational perspectives and models.

Moving away from the literature to my research in Wales over recent years, three main themes have been identified as integral to the management challenges faced by middle managers operating in collaborative settings. The theoretical and empirical literature offers a wide range of factors, approaches and behaviours involved in managing for collaboration, but these three themes constitute the essence of the challenge. They are – managing for common purpose, managing complexity and interdependency and managing relationships – intimately connected, dynamic and crucial to the effectiveness of the middle manager's endeavours. Agency, of course, cannot be disconnected from 'structure', and the empowering or disabling effects of structural factors such as organisational configurations, legislative and statutory duties, financial frameworks, culture and systems of accountability and performance. The influence and impact of some of these have been touched on in part during the course of the discussion, but the analysis has been generated primarily from the viewpoint of the middle managers. This resonates with the assertion of O'Leary et al (2012: S81) that: 'individuals are the strongest factor in whether a collaboration is catalysed or hindered'.

Certainly, framing common purpose – the reasons why people and agencies contemplate working together, the various motivations that drive their engagement, the outcomes they anticipate, their understandings of collaboration, and its machinery and processes – must be the central and constant preoccupations of middle managers engaged in this form of governance. Managing competing motivations, which are invariably dynamic, changing as a result of the course of the collaboration itself as well as responding to external influences relating to budgets and priorities, is a constant headache; as is balancing woolly and aspirational visions which might be catalytic and consensual with more concrete and realisable outcomes that clearly commit individual collaborative agents. It demands a mindset from middle managers that is willing to embrace diversity, and an ability to be 'multi-lensed' – to see the world through the eyes of partners. Professional and organisational prejudices need to be parked to allow frames and understandings of the shared policy world to be learned. This process needs 'safe spaces', mostly facilitated through personal relationships and networks, rather than formal and set piece occasions. Appreciating other people's viewpoints, of course, does not necessarily mean embracing them totally, particularly if they are at odds with an employing organisation's interests, but they constitute the basis upon which a shared course of action might be negotiated. In many ways, collaboration is a means of realising individual self-interests. The fruits of collaboration can be unevenly shared by participants, but over time there must be sufficient benefits for each to ensure sustainability.

One cannot underestimate the fact that managing in collaboration is a highly complex and problematic business. Problems and issues cannot be managed through professional and agency tunnels because they spill over dynamically into multiple relationships and interdependencies. Problem causes, solutions, interventions and impacts intermingle in a 'public policy soup'. Middle managers brought up on a diet of managing a set of duties and policies relating to particular functions must be able to demonstrate an analytical ability to envisage and appreciate a wider backcloth. This is frequently referred to as the 'jigsaw' – a pattern of relationships and connections between managers, organisations, policies, budgets, problems and interventions. This constitutes the knowledge base of collaboration, and a key question is whether it can be taught or primarily acquired through the experience of working in collaboration and being wired into relevant local networks. There is little doubt that middle managers who have worked together in a particular area benefit from accumulated knowledge and experience that might be specific to a particular geographical or policy area but might be transferable more widely. In addition to knowledge about connections, relationships and interdependencies, middle managers benefit from having a degree of knowledge about what other partner agencies do, as well as being proficient in their own area of competence or professional expertise. Processes of learning and knowledge management are a central underpinning to gaining an understanding and insight into a collaborative policy framework. A key issue is whether to allow such mechanisms and processes to occur in a spontaneous and unplanned fashion, or to subject them to critical and planned strategies and interventions.

Completing the trio of factors that represent the essence of managing in collaboration is the management of relationships – the type and quality of the personal and professional interactions that are necessary to manage effectively in this form of governance. Their importance is magnified because the underlying power relationships between actors are not so much grounded in traditional sources relating to position and control of budgets and staff, but more in an ability to share, and work with others more equally on matters of seeking common purpose and devising joint solutions. Influencing is important based on an ability to understand complexity and interdependencies, and to frame common purpose to encompass the self-interests of different parties. Building and sustaining a network of relationships helps to build social capital in a collaborative system. The thorny and contested notion of trust is a key factor mediating such relationships, and the importance of having the 'right' person in collaborative arenas is frequently highlighted, suggestive of the ability of middle managers to project positive personality traits and behaviours relating to openness, transparency and empathy. The importance of managing relationships spills over into the leadership component of a middle manager's collaborative role, translating into styles and approaches that foster shared, distributed and dispersed leadership models.

Having outlined the main components of management in collaboration, Chapter 6 confronts the perennial question of whether this form of management is any different to that practised within organisations, and if so, in what way. Sadly, there is little consensus on this matter with positions polarised between the two extremes and various others occupying a more middle ground. Perhaps it is possible to agree that the challenges faced in collaboration are of a magnitude and severity greater than those confronting single organisations. Perhaps even, that the basic tools of management are broadly similar between the two contexts, and it is essentially a matter of careful judgement which ones to use.

A National Academy of Public Administration Report (2007: 85) published over a decade ago commented that:

> In 1979, the world was much less chaotic and complex, more placid and predictable…at least in relative terms. And the various problems that faced our nation then could more or less fit into their neat bureaucratic boxes, where government technocrats could go about solving them. In that bygone world, deep functional, technical, and organisational specialization was a good thing, and narrow, agency-centric, or functionally specific career paths were the norm. Today, we refer to those specialised career paths as stovepipes – or 'cylinders of excellence' – but they've proven remarkably resistant to change.

Another decade on, and it might equally be argued that management in public services still remains highly functional and professionalised in nature, making it difficult to react to the complexities inherent in a highly interdependent and connected world. A considerable amount of organisational design continues to focus on creating structures, systems and roles that achieve relatively fixed organisational roles and fit well with other structural elements of the organisation. Critically, this approach does not address the highly dynamic, non-linear boundary spanning work facing modern public agencies. Allred et al (2011: 151) take the view that:

> entrenched organisational structures and cultures perpetuate interfirm and interorganisational conflict and stifle collaboration. Yet, although these barriers are pervasive, efforts to remove them tend to be piecemeal and isolated. Boundary spanning initiatives like aligning goals and metrics, improving information sharing, and investing in collaborative people skills are seldom embraced holistically. The failure to take a holistic approach to developing a collaboration capability often sows the seeds of cynicism toward future initiatives.

It is difficult to fathom the reasoning behind an educational, training and development portfolio that remains committed to producing functionally specialised, professional public managers not geared to working in collaborative forms of governance. Why should it be the case that middle managers often have to learn through experience rather than training, and to reject or moderate management approaches and practices that were previously embedded in them for intra-organisational settings?

One middle manager (Williams, 2017) commented that the challenge of developing future middle managers who are comfortable with managing in collaborative settings is dependant upon attracting those "who can deal with change without feeling threatened – who see collaboration as an opportunity rather than a threat" and "of creating networks of such people who can work across boundaries – providing them with space and skills to work jointly because the position of boundaries is not the issue, rather it is their ability to work through and across them". Other contributors referred to the need for middle managers not to be: "status conscious" or influenced by "the organisational ranking of partners"; or to be "too professionalized and narrowly focused". It was felt that a narrow adherence to individual professional practices with the accompanying tendency to impose ideas and methods on others was counterproductive, and the difficult balance was to remain cognisant of professional standards but not a slave to them, in order to appreciate and learn from other equally relevant viewpoints. One school of thought may be that not all middle managers have the capacity or inclination to manage effectively in collaboration. Indeed, there is evidence that particular middle managers flourish in this kind of environment and are motivated and excited by the variety, diversity, challenges and rewards on offer – which can be materially different from the mundane and repetitive tasks associated with managing within professional roles. This obviously is influenced by competence and ability but might also reflect personality types and the capacity to operate in complex and ambiguity-ridden environments. The pen-pictures of effective middle managers operating in collaboration illustrated in Chapter 4 add testament to this view.

Acknowledging that there is an appetite from policy makers and practitioners for concise prescriptions of how to intervene and manage effectively in the design and delivery of public services, Box 8.1 is a summary of the main lessons that have been distilled from the preparation of this book for middle managers working in collaboration. Great care needs to be taken with this list as it is intended only as a guide or checklist of factors that need to be taken into account when devising policies and strategies in this policy area.

Box 8.1: Ten key lessons for middle managers working in collaboration

• Managing in collaboration demands a particular approach and set of behaviours; some of these may also be relevant working within organisations particularly corporate and inter-departmental activities.

- Managing in collaboration requires skilful management based on knowledge, experience, expertise, skills and competencies, especially building and sustaining effective personal and professional relationships including networks; facilitating and working in teams; communication and conflict resolution; influencing, negotiating and consensus seeking in pursuit of shared purposes; having collaborative knowledge based on connections and interdependencies.
- The leadership element of a collaborating middle manager needs to be premised on shared, dispersed and distributed approaches.
- The ability to recognise and balance the multiple accountabilities, tensions and dilemmas stemming from personal, professional, organisational and collaborative sources, need to be cultivated.
- An effective collaborating middle manager has the ability to understand, articulate and assess the implications of the framing processes of partners, especially their motivations and desired outcomes.
- The nature of collaboration requires middle managers to be tolerant of heighted sources of risk, and a propensity to demonstrate innovation and creativity.
- Middle managers working in collaboration need to be developed and supported by an effective education, training and development programme. This might include inter-professional training, formal education programmes, mentoring, secondments, job rotations and communities of practice.
- Mechanisms need to be devised to motivate, incentivise, performance manage and reward middle managers working in collaboration.
- Middle managers need to recognise that they have a critical role to play in both the formulation and delivery of collaborative outcomes – influencing the shape of the collaborative effort as a whole, and ensuring that their own organisations are receptive to, and fit for purpose, for their own organisational challenges.
- While this list primarily concerns agency – the role of middle managers – their role and management needs to be set within a supportive and enabling collaborative infrastructure of policies, coordinating mechanisms, financial frameworks, accountability and performance structures and culture.

An interesting question also relates to whether or not there is a significant measure of distinctiveness and difference in the role and management of middle managers compared with other types of manager. Setting aside the definitional challenges of delineating the concept of a middle manager, the main source of their singularity stems from their positional locus within organisations which foregrounds their intermediary role between top and senior management, and staff and practitioners closer to the frontline of service delivery and provision. This is both potentially catalytic in being able to shape the design and delivery of services, but also somewhat invidious by virtue of being sandwiched between the often-different interests and priorities of senior management and frontline practitioners, resulting in unenviable and multiple accountabilities. Arguably, there is no other group of managers who have the potential and means to influence both the planning and organisation of services, and the practicalities of service delivery. Organisations, in the main, look to middle managers to make things happen – to convert policy intention and strategy into policy delivery. The tools they have to make this happen are financial budgets and HR responsibilities – and they are increasingly held to account through various performance management regimes. Along with other managers, middle managers are able to undertake their duties with the aid of a battery of organisational rules, policies, practices and protocols, sedimented within a scaffolding of organisational and structural architecture. What is important is that a middle manager is in a position to significantly influence the work of an organisation – whether to be 'a safe pair of hands' to ensure the efficient and effective delivery of services, or whether, indeed, to embrace risk and innovation, and look to respond to the challenges of a changing policy environment, including working in collaboration. This latter route severely tests the normal practices and behaviours of organisations, and certainly demands the deployment of a particular set of competencies and management behaviours by middle managers. Some of these – building networks and relationships, understanding interdependencies and negotiation skills – might already have been sharpened within the processes of inter-departmental working. However, these are systematised within the unifying authority structure of a single organisation, and are not necessarily sufficient and robust to cope with the particular challenges of working with other agencies where power and control is diffuse, the emphasis is on securing common purpose, sharing resources and influence is paramount, and ceding authority for a common good must be a realistic expectation. An earlier chapter examined whether managing between organisations is in a way different to that within organisations – a question that has attracted different opinions by researchers and academics. While there may be some consensus on the fact that middle managers often use a similar set of management tools and practices to underpin their work in both contexts – albeit in different permutations and intensities – the skilfulness with which they deploy them is critical to their effectiveness. In my research interviews, countless examples were given of middle managers who appeared just to 'be going through the motions' of working in collaboration, more concerned with protecting their own organisation from having 'to give things up' or share, and patently not equipped with the skills and competencies required to work in a collaborative context. In sharp contrast, the value of having middle managers who appreciated the benefits of collaborative working both for their own agencies and for the system as a whole, and were highly proficient in the management behaviours and skills necessary to underpin their involvement, was greatly respected. The distinctiveness of this cadre of middle manager lies in its capability to manage effectively with a collaboration, together with maintaining and influencing the interests and groups within their home organisations – both at senior management level and frontline practitioners and administrators.

Returning to the discussion with regard to whether middle managers are thrown into the deep end of collaborative working to sink or swim, or whether they can be identified and trained in preparation for such a form of management, a rational approach suggests the latter strategy. The implications of a focus on middle managers operating in collaborative settings for policy, practice and learning are considerable. They have ramifications for the design and delivery of education, training, professional and managerial development. Formal undergraduate and postgraduate training needs to reflect far more the challenges and nuances of managing in collaboration underpinned by both relevant theoretical and empirical perspectives. Business schools in particular might be encouraged to embrace the realities of a tri-sector context rather than perpetuate its narrow focus on the private sector. Individual professions represented in public management need to check out whether they are producing professionals who are fit for the purpose of managing in collaborative settings, and inter- and multi-professional education and training needs to be encouraged in order to prepare future managers for the diverse boundary challenges which they will inevitably be required to confront. Aside from formal education, practising middle managers need to be afforded development and training opportunities to ensure that they have the appropriate skills and abilities to manage effectively in collaboration. Chapter 7 includes a number of frameworks consisting of broadly similar competencies that have been developed to assist with this process. Also, given the importance of personal networking and building social capital, the value of encouraging communities of practice and shared learning opportunities between collaborating middle managers should be encouraged.

Knowledge gaps and a future research and evaluation agenda

This thrust of this book underscores the need for more research, both theoretical and empirical, on the role, nature and behaviours of middle managers operating in theatres of collaboration. The perpetual growth of collaboration across the breadth of public services is unlikely to abate, highlighting the importance of understanding the most effective and efficient ways of designing and delivering public policy within this form of governance. Both theory and practice have traditionally been grounded within single organisational forms, although a growing body of evidence has been accumulated within other contexts. This, however, is insufficient in many areas, including the role of middle managers. It has been argued that their contribution to the course and outcomes of collaboration are potentially pivotal for a number of reasons, but robust theoretical and empirical evidence is relatively embryonic with some notable exceptions. A future research agenda needs to embrace this challenge as a matter of some urgency, positioning it within a structure–agency framework because of the highly interconnected relationships between them. The structural components need to reflect the myriad of forms that collaboration takes – at different levels, intensities, structures, purposes and sectoral combinations – designed to tackle a wide range of public problems and issues. The agential influences need to deconstruct the general category of 'middle manager' and work towards a clearer understanding of who exactly might be included. There are different types of middle manager working in different public agencies with different sets of responsibilities in terms of department, professional background and role. Research agendas need to be sensitive to these structural and agential variations to search for both robust theoretical explanations, and evidence-based practice and policy to inform the design and delivery of ongoing and future collaborations. In general, the training and development of current and potential middle managers is not well developed and tailored to the needs of an integral component of future public management. A more developed and nuanced understanding and appreciation of the type of management required by middle managers in collaboration would inform this education and management training deficiency.

The research questions that need to explored by a future agenda include:

• What is the role of a middle manager working in collaboration?
• What are the key components of management in collaboration in terms of approach, style and behaviour?
• What abilities, skills and competencies do middle managers need to be effective in collaboration?
• What mechanisms are appropriate to evaluate the performance and impact of middle managers working in collaboration?
• What strategies and tactics are used by middle managers to balance the conflicting pressures and tensions of managing both within their own organisations and in collaboration?

- What are the implications of middle managers operating in collaboration for their education, training and development?

The design of future research approaches to answer such questions can be varied and flexible, but opportunities to ground them in the practical working lives and experiences of middle managers would be illuminating. This suggests more qualitative methods – ethnographic and critical incident methodologies to reflect the understandings of middle managers themselves; action-research to explore the impact of middle manager's interventions and behaviours; and case studies to reflect a wide range of contexts and policy areas/problems within which middle managers perform. There is a tendency for government to default to structural solutions to promote and encourage cross-agency collaboration – re-organisations and re-structurings, statutory duties and financial incentives – rather than to investigate mechanisms and policies that might facilitate the effective role and performance of middle managers in this environment. Politicians herald structural interventions as the immediate antidote to systems failure, whereas an investment in agency and cultural change does not necessarily reap the speedy transformations envisaged. Arguably, this is a misguided view because an appropriate investment in agency is more likely to deliver longer term and sustainable success. Middle managers in my research were consistently of the view that although certain structures help and hinder collaboration in various ways – enable or inhibit managerial and professional actions – in the end, it is the commitment and competence of middle managers that make or break collaborative practices.

An additional stream of future research would usefully be directed towards the evaluation and impact of the diverse training and development programmes that are associated with improving collaboration competence and capabilities. As a general observation, it is often quite challenging to secure effective training and development opportunities in the first instance, largely because of the perceived resource implications in relation to other priorities, let alone design evaluation and impact studies to support them. The impact of training and development programmes can be gauged over different time scales – short, medium and long terms – and at different levels or scales. The challenge of designing and funding evaluation and impact studies will vary over different time frames – certainly, it will influence the research methodologies that are used. There will also be differential expectations from the various interests involved in the research findings – policy makers and practitioners are likely to be more interested in early lessons and learning of the 'what works' variety, so favouring short-term studies. Academics are more likely to promote longer-term studies to fully evaluate the impact of training and development initiatives over an extended period of time. These positions are not easy to reconcile when it comes to securing funding.

In terms of impact, it needs to be recognised that this can be evaluated at broadly four different levels – individual, organisational, collaborative and systems. At an individual level, it is about gauging the changes that a training or development intervention has had on the personal competency and capability of a middle manager – about taking a baseline before the intervention, and assessing its impact following it. At an organisational level, it concerns the impact that the training of individual middle managers or a group of middle managers has had on the structure, culture, performance and capability of an organisation to work in collaboration. Have the training programmes enabled host organisations to work more effectively in collaboration as a result of the improved skills of their middle managers? Allred et al (2011: 133) argue that: 'adroit collaboration skills reduce counterproductive behavior by promoting goal alignment, more frequent and open information sharing, higher levels of managerial interaction, the exchange of expertise and resources, and a willingness to share risks and rewards'. So, evaluation studies at an organisational level need to address the impact of training programmes on these and other related factors to determine whether or not they achieve the outcomes that are desired. Moving up the levels, the impact of training programmes can also be assessed at a collaboration and even systems level. What effect might they have for multi-sector and cross-organisational partnerships, and can their impact be measured across a level of government – local, regional or national?

There are considerable practical and methodological challenges associated with undertaking the kind of evaluation and impact studies envisaged above. They require sustained investment in both time and resources; they need to be integrated into the policymaking process from the outset to ensure that any changes can be gauged; and all stakeholders and interests need to be involved in both the design methodology and utilisation of any evaluation. On the latter point, it is especially important that any intended recipients of evaluation research have the necessary skills to interpret the results. This relates to the broader issue of the problems associated with the acceptability of such research in the light of its limitations in influencing public policy and practice. Timely results, an uncontested methodology, results that reflect existing political philosophies and are reported with low degrees of uncertainty, and that are delivered by skilful research advocates, all increase the chances of it being taken seriously (Percy-Smith et al, 2003).

Final thoughts

Middle managers occupy the beating heart of many organisations – sandwiched between a top tier of Directors and Heads of Service offering leadership, direction and accountability, and a much larger body of practitioners, professionals, administrators and frontline staff who more directly interface with the recipients of public services. Although this standing comes with a certain amount of power in relation to their control over staff and budgets, it can also result in considerable pressure particularly in terms of performance and human resource management. Working in collaboration brings with it an additional burden of difficulty that many middle managers are not normally equipped to manage. Yet, arguably, the challenges of collaboration are of a type and magnitude that demand especially skilful management. It is worth repeating as a salutary reminder that the formal evidence of numerous evaluation studies suggests that the results of collaborative working are far from impressive – particularly in relation to the amount of time and effort that is invested in it. This is further compounded by the many occasions when public inquiries and other forms of scrutiny conclude that 'a failure to work in collaboration between agencies' is a major cause of miscarriages, disasters and fiascoes in public policy and management. The case for preparing middle managers to work effectively in collaboration should be a high priority for public management of the future.

Appendix: questions for discussion

This appendix is designed for use with students, policy makers, managers and practitioners in group discussion sessions such as workshops and learning sets. It is envisaged as a resource for academics and trainers who are keen to explore and facilitate discussion around the themes and topics considered in this book. The questions can be tailored to the needs of particular audiences, and are organised around the material, arguments and content stemming from individual chapters.

Chapter 2

The following questions primarily concern notions of collaboration; the implications of the prevailing policy context; the nature, role and behaviours of middle managers; the skills and competencies of middle managers; inter-departmental working; understanding power and trust; and the challenges of collaborative working.

1. Identify the key features – social, economic, environmental and political – of the prevailing public policy landscape in your area. What are the implications of these for the manner in which public management is approached and organised, and the role that public managers perform?
2. What are the benefits of, and enablers and barriers to collaboration?
3. Is the notion of 'collaboration' clear or are there multiple interpretations of working together with other managers and organisations? Can you devise a typology of relationships, perhaps along a continuum, that characterise different expressions of collaboration?
4. What challenges and barriers do middle managers encounter in the course of discharging their roles and duties?
5. Catalogue and discuss the tensions, ambiguities and challenges of working both within and between organisations, and explore the strategies involved in managing them.
6. Consider the various sources of power you have as a middle manager working within your organisation, and then

compare and contrast these with the sources of power you have working between organisations. Think of examples of how you use them and discuss the issues associated with them.

7. What shape will collaboration take in the future? What forces will drive it and will it increase in its intensity and scope? What will be the implications for approaches to public management?

8. Identify the 'middle managers' in your organisation. Do they constitute a clearly defined group of managers, and if so, what characterises them from other managers in your organisation? Alternatively, is the notion of a 'middle manager' too broad and captures many different types of manager at this level in the organisation?

9. What are the key roles and functions of a 'middle manager', and what are their main sources of power?

10. Set out and discuss the skills and competencies needed to be an effective 'middle manager'. Does an effective 'middle manager' need to have a professional background and experience in the area of policy that he/she is managing, or are generic management skills sufficient to operate in any policy area?

11. Middle managers often have to work with people and teams in many different parts of their organisation. What are the particular challenges and tensions or working in this fashion, and what particular skills and management behaviours are necessary?

12. Think about the interactions and relationships – both formal and informal – you have with other organisations during the course of your work. What form do these take? Do you choose to work in this fashion, or is it mandated in some way by government? Do you consider that working with other organisations is a legitimate part of your job role, and one that is necessary to fulfil your objectives or the objectives of your client group?

13. Is the task of managing within your organisation broadly similar to or different from managing with other organisations? Give reasons for your response.

14. What are the particular challenges, tensions and ambiguities of working with other organisations? Do they relate to power, expertise, culture, ways of working, accountability, resources or what?
15. Are there any particular barriers that inhibit middle managers from working in collaboration, and if so, how might these be overcome?
16. How do you influence people over whom you have no direct power? What strategies and approaches do you use? Give some examples.
17. It is argued that 'trust' is a very important aspect of managing in collaboration. What is your understanding of this notion, and how do you go about building and sustaining it with people in other organisations? Give some examples.
18. Do you consider that a middle manager's personality has to be of a particular type to be effective working in collaboration? Justify your answer. Also, do you consider that women rather than men make better collaborators? Or do middle managers from a particular policy area, sector or age group make better collaborators?
19. How is a 'middle manager' held to account while managing in collaboration? Is that singly to the home organisation, or contemporaneously with the collaboration? How can accountability and performance frameworks be built into a middle manager's appraisal system?
20. Reflect on a collaborative management experience/project that you have been associated with. Has this been successful or not? What reasons can you give for the particular outcome – is it to do with structural/institutional factors, or the way in which managers have worked together?
21. Think about a middle manager that you are aware of that you consider being a model example of an effective collaborator. Justify your decision with an outline of their key characteristics and approach to management.
22. Draw up a job description for a middle manager required to work both within and between organisations. Consider knowledge, experience, skills and personal attributes.

Chapter 3

The questions relating to this chapter concern common purpose; issues connected to vision and mission statements; and framing.

1. What is involved in identifying and negotiating common purpose and how might these be achieved?
2. Interrogate some examples of vision and mission statements and test their validity against the criteria of credibility, ownership, achievability and uniqueness.
3. Think of a collaboration that you have been involved with. Reflect on the way that your 'frames' and those of others have been identified and understood. Has your view of the world been influenced by others and vice versa?
4. What are the underpinning values of each of the following sectors – public, private and third? Can these be reconciled within the context of a collaboration involving the design and delivery of public services, and if so, how?
5. How can the many diverse professional groups involved in health and social care services work together effectively given that their respective 'frames' are often different?
6. Think of a person you have encountered whom you consider is especially skilled in helping other managers understand their frames and the implications of these in a collaborative context? Justify your choice with examples.
7. Devise the framework for a collaborative strategic management process that reflects purpose, direction and outcome.

Chapter 4

The focus of the questions in this section concern appreciating connections and relationships within policy issues; innovation and creativity; learning and knowledge management; and boundary objects.

1. Select a policy issue or problem with which you are familiar. Identify and map the connections and relationships that exist

between organisations that impact on, or are responsible for it. Different stakeholders have different levels of power, what strategies would you use to work with them – consult, inform, collaborate or what?

2. How would you go about making a case for a collaborative approach to any of the following: health and social care; domestic violence; childhood obesity; long-term unemployment; anti-social behaviour; drug and alcohol misuse; poverty?

3. How can middle managers be encouraged to work connectively looking outwards rather through traditional professional and organisational stovepipes with which they are familiar? Are there particular skills they need to discharge this role?

4. Identify a project, plan or policy from your particular area of work based on collaboration that you consider would improve on existing services? Prepare a feasibility study showing how would this would result in an improved service including, why the existing service arrangements are inefficient or lack coherence and co-ordination; how your solutions would be designed to address these; and how you would measure success.

5. It can be argued that making connections between organisations and their responsibilities in a particular shared policy area or problem is a recipe for innovation and creativity. Give some examples of instances where this has occurred, and what do you consider to be the main factors that have contributed to this phenomenon.

6. Select a 'wicked issue' and outline its main characteristics and form in terms of its cross-boundary nature; its multiple social constructions and framing; and its complexity and interrelationships.

7. How can innovation, creativity and entrepreneurship be encouraged and promoted in collaboration? What are the main barriers to these and how might these be managed?

8. What particular competencies and skills do middle managers need to be effective in promoting and demonstrating innovation?

9. Design a learning and knowledge management strategy for a collaboration you are associated with, considering issues such as purpose, levels of learning, barriers and facilitators, types, mechanisms for sharing/transferring, enabling structures and resources.

10. What are the benefits/challenges of bringing together managers from different professions, organisations and sectors, and how have these been tackled? How do managers learn from each other and together on joint issues?

11. How does learning occur, what type of learning is generated (tacit/explicit) and at what level – individual, group or organisational?

12. How would you describe a 'culture of learning' and how can it be developed? How can middle managers create the 'right' conditions for learning and knowledge management in collaboration?

13. Does information and knowledge flow freely between you and middle managers with whom you work in other organisations? How important is trust and personal relationships in this process?

14. What structures and mechanisms do you consider are necessary to promote learning and knowledge management in any collaboration?

15. Would you describe yourself as a 'knowledge champion' or 'broker'? What are the key attributes of such a person?

16. Select a number of different types of 'boundary object' and using Fong et al's (2007) model explore their characteristics and potential role in collaboration?

Chapter 5

The questions stimulated by the discussion from this chapter include the skills and competencies of middle managers working in collaboration; sources of power; trust, accountabilities and the role of personality.

1. Think of an effective middle manager whom you have encountered working in collaboration. Give reasons for your choice and outline the skills and attributes this person uses?

2. Conversely, think of a middle manager who is a poor exponent of managing between organisations, giving reasons for your choice.

3. Using critical incident analysis, think of occasions in collaborative working when your involvement or intervention made a difference either directly or indirectly.

   The critical incident may be one:
   • that went unusually well;
   • which did not go as planned;
   • that was very ordinary and typical;
   • that captures the essence of a particular skill or competency;
   • that was particularly demanding.

   Reflect on the context of the incident; why you consider the incident was critical to you; how you were feeling; what particular competency(s) was involved; how effective you were; and, what lessons and learning were involved.

4. What sources of power do middle managers have when managing within organisations, and how do they use them?

5. What sources of power do middle managers have when managing between organisations, and how do they use them?

6. How do you build and sustain trust with people you work with in other organisations? Can you trust people in other organisations as much as in your own?

7. Who are middle managers accountable to when they manage between organisations? If you consider there are multiple sources of accountability, what problems and tension arise from these and how do you manage them?

8. How important is it to have the 'right' people representing their organisations in a collaborative? Does this happen by chance, or can they be trained and selected?

9. What happens to the dynamics of a collaborative group when key middle managers move away? How is this best managed? Is this healthy for a group in terms of bringing

in new ideas and innovation, or largely a destabilizing influence?

10. Have middle managers got to be of a particular personality type to be effective in collaboration? If so, what behaviours and values need to be displayed?

11. One means of assessing the effectiveness of a collaboration is through the application of a 'health check'. This is designed to assess how well the group and the individuals within it are performing; whether it is fit for purpose; whether there are any problems associated with its organisation and constitution; whether it is achieving its objectives; and, whether it can be improved in any way. Design the framework for a 'health check' on a collaborative group.

Chapter 6

The questions flowing from this chapter concern the distinctiveness of different forms of management; whether they require different skills and competencies; and balancing the roles of intra and inter-organisational working.

1. Do you consider that managing in collaboration constitutes a distinct form of management? If so, how does if differ from other forms of management? If not, which other forms of management can it be compared with?

2. What are the main components of your role while managing in your own organisation? What are the main components of your role while working in a collaborative setting? Are they the same or different? Think of the main skills you use.

3. In terms of the skills and competencies that you possess, do you deploy them equally while working in and between organisations, or are there any that are particularly appropriate in either setting?

4. Does working in collaboration present you with any difficulties when it comes to issues of accountability? If so, how do you manage them?

5. How do you balance your role as a middle manager with your role working in collaboration? Does one take priority

over the other? Do you spend more time on one as opposed to the other?

Chapter 7

The questions in this section revolve around personality characteristics; performance management regimes; incentives and rewards; training and development; communities of practice; inter-professional collaboration; and, the nature of formal education programmes.

1. Can the personal attributes or characteristics of a middle manager be altered or modified, or are these fixed by their individual personality?
2. Design a performance management framework for individual middle managers operating in collaboration. How can you connect the individual performance of middle managers to collaborative outcomes? Is it possible to calculate the value of 'collaborative effort' separately from that of collaborative outcomes, and, if so, how?
3. What measures would you propose to incentivise and reward middle managers for working in collaboration?
4. There are frequent references to the desirability of creating a 'public service ethos' – a set of principles and ethics that are designed to capture the heart of public service provision. Discuss the ways in which a 'collaboration ethos' might be designed, cultivated and sustained in the same way that a 'public service ethos' has been developed over the years.
5. Thinking about your approach to managing in collaboration: how do you react when others' perceptions and understandings of a situation are different from your own? Do you react with irritation or welcome them? How do you influence others – do you push your own ideas at all costs or are you prepared to invite and embrace others?
6. Devise a training and development programme for middle managers operating in collaborative settings. Give details of the methods you propose and how they might best be delivered. Think about how you might assess the competence of middle managers following such a programme.

7. You are charged with setting up a collaborative community of practice for middle managers operating in your local geographical or policy area. Set out how you would go about this task giving details of its potential role and benefits, who it might involve, how it will be organised and the kind of activities that would be arranged. Provide a briefing paper and draft letter of invitation to potential participants.

8. Set out and discuss the measures that an organisation can take to improve its readiness for, and ability to, engage effectively in collaboration.

9. What knowledge and experience does a middle manager have as evidence in support of an application to manage in collaborative settings?

10. What strategies would you propose for encouraging inter-professional collaboration? Should the aim be to cross, merge, re-locate, dissolve or protect the boundaries between different professionals?

11. Design the structure and content of a postgraduate module on 'Working in Collaboration'.

References

6, P., Goodwin, N., Peck, E. and Freeman, T. (2006) *Managing Networks of Twenty-first Century Organizations*, Basingstoke: Palgrave

Addicott, R., McGivern, G. and Ferlie, E. (2006) 'Networks, organizational management: NHS cancer networks', *Public Money and Management*, Vol. 26 (2), pp. 87–94

Agranoff, R. (2003) *Collaborative Public Management: New Strategies for Local Governments*, Washington, DC: Georgetown University Press

Agranoff, R. (2006) 'Inside collaborative networks: Ten lessons for public managers', *Public Administration Review*, Vol. 66 (Special Issue), pp. 55–65

Agranoff, R. (2007) *Managing within Networks: Adding Value to Public Organizations*, Washington, DC: Georgetown University Press

Agranoff, R. (2012) *Collaborating to Manage: A Primer for the Public Sector*, Washington, DC: Georgetown University Press

Agranoff, R. (2013) *Leveraging Networks: A Guide for Public Managers Working across Organizations*, Washington, DC: IBM Endowment for the Business of Government

Agranoff, R. and McGuire, M. (2001) 'Big questions in public sector management research', *Journal of Public Research and Theory*, Vol. 11, pp. 295–326

Alexander, J.A., Comfort, M.E., Weiner B.J. and Bogue, R. (2001) 'Leadership in collaborative community health partnerships', *Nonprofit Management and Leadership*, Vol. 12 (2), pp. 159–175

Allred, C.R., Fawcett, S.E., Wallin, C. and Magnan, G.M. (2011) 'A dynamic collaboration capability as a source of competitive advantage', *Decision Sciences*, Vol. 42 (1), pp. 129–161

Ansell, C. and Torfing, J. (2015) 'How does collaborative governance scale?', *Policy and Politics*, Vol. 43 (3), pp. 315–329

Ansell, C. and Torfing, J. (2017) 'Improving policy implementation through collaborative policy making', *Policy and Politics*, Vol. 45 (3), pp. 467–486

ARACY (Australian Research Alliance for Children and Youth) (2007) *The Impact of Power and Politics in a Complex Environment*, Canberra: ARACY

ARACY (Australian Research Alliance for Children and Youth) (2013a) *Key Elements of Collaboration (Factsheet 5)*, Canberra: ARACY

ARACY (Australian Research Alliance for Children and Youth) (2013b) *Managing Collaborations (Factsheet 8)* Canberra: ARACY

ARACY (Australian Research Alliance for Children and Youth) (2013c) *Collaborative Competencies/Capabilities (Factsheet 14)*, Canberra: ARACY

Argyris, C. and Schon, D. (1996) *Organizational Learning II: Theory, Method and Practice*, Reading: Addison-Wesley

Balogun, J. (2003) 'From blaming the middle to harnessing its potential: Creating change intermediaries', *British Journal of Management*, Vol. 69, pp. 69–83

Balogun, J. (2007) 'The practice of organizational restructuring: From design to reality', *European Management Journal*, Vol. 25 (2), pp. 81–91

Barclay, B.T. (2013) *Developing Senior Executive Capabilities to Address National Priorities*, Washington, DC: IBM Center for the Business of Government

Bardach, E. (1996) 'Turf barriers to interagency collaboration', in D.F. Kettl and H.B. Milward (eds) *The State of Public Management*, Baltimore, MD and London: John Hopkins University Press

Bardach, E. (1998) *Getting Agencies to Work Together*, Washington, DC: Brookings Institution Press

Barrett, M. and Oborn, E. (2010) 'Boundary object use in cross-cultural software development teams', *Human Relations*, Vol. 63 (8), pp.1199–1221

Bate, S.P. and Roberts, G. (2002) 'Knowledge management and communities of practice in the private sector: Lessons for modernizing the National Health Service in England and Wales', *Public Administration*, Vol. 80 (4), pp. 643–663

Benford, R.D. and Snow, D.A. (2000) 'Framing processes and social movements: An overview and assessment', *Annual Review of Sociology*, Vol. 26, pp. 611–639

Bingham, L.B. and O'Leary, R. (2006) 'Conclusion. Parallel play, not collaboration: Missing questions, missing connections', *Public Administration Review*, Vol. 66 (Special Issue), pp. 161–167

Bingham, L.B., Sandfort, J. and O'Leary, R. (2008) 'Learning to do and doing to learn: Teaching managers to collaborate in networks', in L.B. Bingham and R. O'Leary (eds) *Big Ideas in Collaborative Public Management*, Armonk, NY: M.E. Sharpe

Bovaid, T. and Loffler, E. (2003) 'Understanding public management and governance', in T. Bovaid and E. Loffler (eds) *Public Management and Governance*, London: Routledge

Bowker, G. and Star, S.L. (1999) *Sorting Things Out: Classification and Its Consequences*, Cambridge, MA: MIT Press

Boyatzis, R. (1982) *The Competent Manager*, London: Wiley

Brown, J.S. and Duguid, P. (1991) 'Organizational learning and communities-of-practice: Toward a unified view of working, learning and innovation', *Organization Science*, Vol. 2 (1), pp. 40–57.

Bryson, J. M. and Crosby, B.C. (1992) *Leadership for the Common Good: Tackling Public Problems in a Shared World*, San Francisco, CA: Jossey-Bass

Cairney, P. (2018) 'Three habits of successful policy entrepreneurs', *Policy and Politics*, Vol. 46 (2), pp. 199–215

Canadian Heath Services Research Foundation (2007) *Community of Practice Design Guide: A Step-by-step Guide for Creating Collaborative Communities of Practice*, Issue 33, p.1

Carey, C., Jacobs, K., Malbon, E., Buck, F., Li, A., and Williams, P. (2019) 'Boundary spanners: Towards a Theory of Practice', in Craven, L., Dickinson, H., and Carey, J. (eds) *Crossing Boundaries in Public Policy: Tacking the Critical Challenges*, London: Routledge, pp. 121-134

Carlile, P.R. (2004) 'Transferring, translating, and transforming: An integrative framework for managing knowledge across boundaries', *Organization Science*, Vol. 15 (5), 555–568

Center for State, Tribal and Territorial Support (2012) *Communities of Practice Resource Kit*, Atlanta, GA: US Department of Health and Human Services

Child, J. (2003) 'Learning through strategic alliances', in M. Dierkes, A. Berthoin Antal, J. Child and I. Nonaka (eds) *Handbook of Organizational Learning and Knowledge*, pp. 657–680, Oxford University Press: Oxford

Child, J. (2006) *Organization: Contemporary Principles and Practices*, Oxford: Blackwell Publishing

Child, J., Faulkner, D. and Tallman, S. (2005) *Cooperative Strategy: Managing Alliances, Networks, and Joint Ventures*, Oxford: Oxford University Press

Chrislip, D.D. and Larson, C.E. (1994) *Collaborative Leadership*, San Francisco, CA: Jossey-Bass

CIHC (Canadian Interprofessional Health Collaborative) (2010) *A National Interprofessional Competency Framework*, Vancouver: CIHC, University of British Columbia

Clarke, C., Hope-Hailey, V. and Kelliher, C. (2007) 'Being real or really being someone else? Change, managers and emotion work', *European Management Journal*, Vol. 25 (2), pp. 92–103

Cohen, W.M. and Levinthal, D.A. (1990) 'Absorptive capacity: A new perspective on learning and innovation', *Administrative Science Quarterly*, Vol. 85 (1), pp. 128–152

Connelly, D.R., Zhang, J. and Faerman, S.R. (2008) 'The paradoxical nature of collaboration', in L.B. Bingham and R. O'Leary (eds) *Big Ideas in Collaborative Public Management*, Armonk, New York: M.E. Sharpe

Cook, A. (2015) *Partnership Working Across UK Public Services*, Edinburgh: What Works Scotland

Crosby, B.C. and Bryson, J.M. (2005) *Leadership for the Common Good: Tackling Public Problems in a Shared Power World*, San Francisco, CA: Jossey-Bass

Crossan, M.M., Lane, H.W. and White, R.E. (1999) 'An organizational learning framework: From intuition to institution', *Journal of Management Studies*, Vol. 24 (3), pp. 522–537

Currie, G. and Procter, S.J. (2005) 'The antecedents of middle managers' strategic contribution: The case of a professional bureaucracy', *Journal of Management Studies*, Vol. 42 (7), pp. 1325–1356

Currie, G. and Suhomliova, O. (2006) 'The impact of institutional forces upon knowledge sharing in the UK NHS: the triumph of professional power and the inconsistency of power', *Public Administration*, Vol. 84 (1), pp. 1-30

Dalkir, K. (2011) *Knowledge Management in Theory and Practice*, Boston, MA: Massachusetts Institute of Technology Press

D'Amour, D. and Oandasan, I. (2005) 'Interprofessionality as the field of interprofessional practice and interprofessional education: An emerging concept', *Journal of Interprofessional Care*, Supplement 1, pp. 8–20

De Leeuw, E. and Browne, J. (2018) 'Overlaying structure and frames in policy networks to enable effective boundary spanning', *Evidence and Policy*, Vol. 4 (3), pp. 537–547

De Long, D.W. and Fahey, L. (2000) 'Diagnosing cultural barriers to knowledge management', *Academy of Management Executive*, Vol. 14 (4), pp. 113–127

Dickinson, H. and Carey, G. (2016) *Managing and Leading in Inter-Agency Settings*, Bristol: Policy Press

Donahue, J. (2004) 'On collaborative governance', *Working Paper No. 2*, Cambridge, MA: John F. Kennedy School of Government

Donahue, J. and Zeckhauser, R.J. (2008) 'Public-Private Collaboration', in Moran, M., Rein, M., and Goodin, R.E. (eds) *The Oxford Handbook of Public Policy*, Oxford: Oxford University Press

Du Gay, P. (2005) *The Values of Bureaucracy*, Oxford: Oxford University Press

Dunlop, C.A. and Radaelli, C.M. (2018) 'The lessons of policy learning: Types, triggers, hindrances and pathologies', *Policy and Politics*, Vol. 46 (2), pp. 255–272

Emerson, K. and Smutco, S. (2011) *UNCG Guide to Collaborative Competency*, Portland, OR: Policy Consensus Initiative and University Network for Collaborative Governance.

Feldman, M.S. and Khademian, A.M. (2007) 'The role of the public manager in inclusion: Creating communities of practice', *Governance: An International Journal of Policy, Administration, and Institutions*, Vol. 20 (2), pp. 305–324

Feldman, M.S., Khademian, A.M., Ingram, H. and Schneider, A.S. (2006) 'Ways of knowing and inclusive management practices', *Public Management Review*, Vol. 66 (Special Issue), pp. 89–99

Floyd, S.W. and Wooldridge, B. (1994) 'Dinosaurs of dynamos? Recognizing middle manager's strategic role', *Academy of Management Executive*, Vol. 8 (4), pp. 47–57

Floyd, S.W. and Wooldridge, B. (1997) 'Middle management's strategic influence and organizational performance', *Journal of Management Studies*, 34(3), pp. 465–485

Floyd, S.W. and Wooldridge, B. (2000) *Building Strategy from the Middle: Reconceptualizing Strategy Process*. London: Sage

Flynn, N. (2002) *Public Sector Management*. Harlow: Pearson

Fong, A., Valerdi, R. and Srinivasan, J. (2007) 'Boundary objects as a framework to understand the role of systems integrators', *Systems Research Forum*, Vol. 2, pp. 11–18

Fountain, J. (2013) *Implementing Cross-Agency Collaboration: A Guide for Federal Managers*, Washington, DC: IBM Centre for Business of Government

Fox, N.J. (2011) 'Boundary objects, social meanings and the success of new technologies', *Sociology*, Vol. 45 (1), pp. 70–85

Friedman, R.A. and Podolny, J. (1992) 'Differentiation of boundary spanning roles: Labor negotiations and implications for role conflict', *Administrative Science Quarterly*, Vol. 37, pp. 28–47

Friedman, V.J. (2001) 'The individual as agent of organizational learning', in M. Dierkes, A. Berthoin Antal, J. Child and I. Nonaka (eds) *Handbook of Organizational Learning and Knowledge*, Oxford: Oxford University Press

Fulop, L. and Linstead, S. (2004) 'Introduction: A critical approach to management and organization', in L. Fulop, S. Linstead, and S. Lilley (eds) *Management and Organization: A Critical Text*, Basingstoke: Palgrave Macmillan

Gajda, R. (2004) 'Utilizing collaboration theory to evaluate strategic alliances', *American Journal of Evaluation*, Vol. 25 (1), pp. 65–77

Gallagher, T. (2008) *Learning In and For Interagency Working: Multiagency Work in Northern Ireland. Full Research Report ESRC End of Award Report*, RES-139-25-0159, Swindon: ESRC

GAO (United States Government Accountability Office) (2005) *Results-Orientated Government: Practices that Can Help Enhance and Sustain Collaboration Among Federal Agencies*, Washington, DC: GAO

GAO (United States Government Accountability Office) (2010) *National Security: An Overview of Professional Development Activities Intended to Improve Interagency Collaboration*, Washington, DC: GAO

GAO (United States Government Accountability Office) (2012a) *Managing for Results: Key Considerations for Implementing Interagency Collaborative Mechanisms*, Washington, DC: GAO

GAO (United States Government Accountability Office) (2012b) *Interagency Collaboration: State and Army Rotation Programs Can Build on Positive Results with Additional Preparation and Evaluation*, Washington, DC: GAO

GAO (United States Government Accountability Office) (2014) *Managing for Results: Implementation Approaches Used to Enhance Collaboration in Interagency Groups*, Washington, DC: GAO

Getha-Taylor, H. (2008) 'Identifying collaborative competencies', *Review of Public Personnel Administration*, Vol. 28 (2), pp. 103–119

Goldsmith, S. and Eggers, W.D. (2004) *Governing by Network: The New Shape of the Public Sector*, Washington, D.C: Brookings Institution Press

Government of South Australia (2016a) *Working Together for Joined-Up Policy Delivery: Project Summary*, Adelaide: Government of South Australia

Government of South Australia (2016b) *Working Together for Joined-Up Policy Delivery Report: Creating Better Outcomes for South Australians Through Joined-Up Policy Delivery*, Adelaide: Government of South Australia

Government of South Australia (2016c) *Working Together: Joined-Up Policy Guide*, Adelaide: Government of South Australia

Gronn, P. (2002) 'Distributed leadership as a unit of analysis', *Leadership Quarterly*, Vol. 13, pp. 423–451

Haneberg, L. (2010) *High Impact Middle Management: Solutions for Today's Busy Public-Sector Managers*, Alexandria, VA: ASTD Press

Hanf, K. I. and Scharpf, F. W. (1978) *Interorganizational Policymaking: Limits to Coordination and Central Government*, London: Sage

Hannah, S.T. and Lester, P.B. (2009) 'A multilevel approach to building and leading learning organizations', *Leadership Quarterly*, Vol. 20, pp. 34–48.

Hardy, C., Phillips, N. and Lawrence, T. (1998) 'Distinguishing trust and power in interorganizational relations: Forms and facades of trust', in C. Lane and R. Bachmann (eds) *Trust In and Between Organizations*, Oxford: Oxford University Press

Health Innovation Network (2015) *Communities of Practice*, London: Health Innovation Network

Heclo, H. (1979) 'Issue Networks and the Executive Establishment', in King, A. (ed) *The New American Political System*, Washington, DC: American Institute for Public Policy Research, pp. 87–124

Herranz, J. (2008) 'The multisectoral trilemma of network management', *Journal of Public Administration Research and Theory*, Vol. 18 (1), pp. 1–31

Hibbert, P., Huxham, C. and Smith Ring, P. (2008) 'Managing collaborative inter-organizational relations', in S. Cropper, M. Ebers, C. Huxham and P. Smith Ring (eds) *The Oxford Handbook of Inter-Organizational Relations*, Oxford: Oxford University Press

Hirsh, W. and Bevan, S. (1988) *What Makes a Manager*, Brighton: University of Brighton

Hirsch, W. and Strebler, M. (1994) 'Defining managerial skills and competencies', in A. Mumford (ed.) *Gower Handbook of Management Development*, Aldershot: Gower

Holland, J.H. (2014) *Complexity: A Very Short Introduction*, Oxford: Oxford University Press

Hupe, P., Hill, M. and Buffat, A. (2016) *Understanding Street Level Bureaucracy*, Bristol: Policy Press

Huy, Q.N. (2002) 'Emotional balancing of organizational continuity and radical change: The contribution of middle managers', *Administrative Science Quarterly*, Vol. 47 (1), pp. 31–69

Huysman M. (1999) 'Balancing biases: A critical review of the literature on organizational learning', in M. Easterby-Smith, J. Burgoyne and L. Araujo (eds) *Organizational Learning and the Learning Organization: Developments in Theory and Practice*, pp. 59–74, Sage: London

Ingraham, P.W. and Getha-Taylor, H. (2008) 'Incentivizing collaborative performance: Aligning policy intent, design and impact', in L.B. Bingham and R. O'Leary (eds) *Big Ideas in Collaborative Public Management*, London: M.E. Sharpe

Inkpen, A. (2000) 'Learning through joint ventures: A framework of knowledge acquisition', *Journal of Management Studies*, Vol. 37 (7), pp. 1019–1043

IPEC (Interprofessional Education Collaborative) (2011) *Core Competences for Interprofessional Practice: Report of an Expert Panel*, Washington, DC: IPEC

IPEC (Interprofessional Education Collaborative) (2016) *Core Competences for Interprofessional Practice: 2016 Update*, Washington, DC: IPEC

Jacobs, R. (1989) 'Getting the measure of managerial competence', *Personnel Management*, Vol. 21 (6) June, pp. 32–37

Jansen, J.J.P., Vera, D. and Crossan, M. (2009) 'Strategic leadership for exploration and exploitation: The moderating role of environmental dynamism', *Leadership Quarterly*, Vol. 20, pp. 5–18

Kanter, R.M. (1997) 'World-class leaders', in F. Hesselbein, M. Goldsmith and R. Beckhard (eds) *The Leader of the Future*, San Francisco, CA: Jossey-Bass

Katz, R.L. (1974) 'Skills of an effective administrator', *Harvard Business Review*, Vol. 52, pp. 90–102

Kelman, S., Hong, S. and Turbitt, I. (2012) 'Are there managerial practices associated with the outcomes of an interagency service delivery collaboration? Evidence from British crime and disorder reduction partnerships', *Journal of Public Administration Research and Theory*, Vol. 23, pp. 609–630

Kerr, P. (2018) *Greeks Bearing Gifts*, London: Quercus

Kickert, W.J.M., Klijn, E.-K. and Koppenjan, J.F.M. (1997) *Managing Complex Networks: Strategies for the Public Sector*, London: Sage

Kingdon, J. (1984) *Agendas, Alternatives and Public Policies*, New York: Harper Collins

Klijn, E.-K. (2005) 'Networks and inter-organizational management: Challenging, steering, evaluation, and the role of public actors in public management', in E. Ferlie, L.E. Lynn and C. Pollitt (eds) *The Oxford Handbook of Public Management*, Oxford: Oxford University Press

Klijn, E.-K. (2008) 'Policy and implementation networks: Managing complex interactions', in S. Cropper, M. Ebers, C. Huxham and P. Smith Ring (eds) *The Oxford Handbook of Inter-Organizational Relations*, Oxford: Oxford University Press

Knoepfel, P., Larrue, C., Varone, F. and Hill, M. (2011) *Public Policy Analysis*, Bristol: Policy Press

Kodner, D.L. and Spreeuwenberg, C. (2002) 'Integrated care: Meaning, logic, applications, and implications – a discussion paper', *International Journal of Integrated Care*, Vol. 2 (14), pp. 1–6

Kolb, D.A. (1984) *Experiential Learning: Experience as the Source of Learning and Development*, Englewood Cliffs, NJ: Prentice Hall

Kooiman, J. (2000) 'Societal governance: Levels, modes, and orders of socio-political interaction', in J. Pierre (ed.) *Debating Governance*, Oxford: Oxford University Press

Kotter, J.P. (1990) *A Force for Change: How Leadership Differs from Management*, London: The Free Press

Lane, C. (1998) 'Introduction: Theories and issues in the study of trust', in C. Lane and R. Bachmann (eds) *Trust In and Between Organizations*, Oxford: Oxford University Press

Lane, C. (2003) 'Organizational learning in supplier networks', in M. Dierkes, A. Berthoin Antal, J. Child and I. Nonaka (eds) *Handbook of Organizational Learning and Knowledge,* pp. 699–715, Oxford: Oxford University Press

Lane, C. and Bachmann, R. (eds) *Trust In and Between Organizations*, Oxford: Oxford University Press

Lane, P.J. and Lubatkin, M. (1998) 'Relative absorptive capacity and inter-organizational learning', *Strategic Management Review*, Vol. 19, pp. 461–477

Lank, E. (2006) *Collaborative Advantage: How Organizations Win by Working Together*, Basingstoke: Palgrave Macmillan

LaPalombara, J. (2003) 'Power and politics in organizations: Public and private sector comparisons', in M. Dierkes, A. Berthoin Antal, J. Child and I. Nonaka (eds) *Handbook of Organizational Learning and Knowledge*, pp. 557–581, Oxford University Press: Oxford

La Porte, T.R. (1996) 'Shifting vantage and conceptual puzzles in understanding public organization networks', *Journal of Public Administration Research and Theory*, Vol. 6 (1), pp. 49–74

Lawrence, T.B., Hardy, C. and Phillips, N. (2002) 'The institutional effects of interorganizational collaboration: the emergence of proto-institutions', *Academy of Management Journal*, Vol. 55 (1), pp. 281–290

Linden, R.M. (2010) *Leading Across Boundaries: Creating Collaborative Agencies in a Networked World*, San Francisco, CA: Jossey-Bass

Lipsky, M. (1980) *Street-level Bureaucracy: Dilemmas of the Individual in Public Services*, New York: Russell Sage Foundation

Lowndes, V. and Skelcher, C. (1998) 'The dynamics of multi-organizational partnerships: An analysis of changing modes of governance', *Local Government Studies*, Vol. 30, pp. 313–333

Lowndes, V. and Squires, S. (2012) 'Cuts, collaboration and creativity', *Public Money and Management*, November, pp. 401–408

Luke, J.S. (1998) *Catalytic Leadership: Strategies for an Interconnected World*, San Francisco, CA: Jossey Bass

Lynn, L.E. (2006) *Public Management: Old and New*, London: Routledge

Mabery, M.J., Gibbs-Scharf, L. and Bara, D. (2013) 'Communities of practice foster collaboration across public health', *Knowledge Management*, Vol. 17 (2), pp. 226–236

Mayer, M. and Smith, A. (2007) 'The practice of change: Understanding the role of middle managers, emotions and tools', *European Management Journal*, Vol. 25 (2), pp. 79–80

McConnell, A. (2018) 'Rethinking wicked problems as political problems and policy problems', *Policy and Politics*, Vol. 46 (1), pp. 165–180

McGuire, M. (2002) 'Managing networks: Propositions on what managers do and why?', *Public Administration Review*, Sept/Oct, Vol. 62 (5), pp. 599–609

McGuire, M. (2006) 'Collaborative public management: Assessing what we know and how we know it', *Public Administration Review*, Vol. 66 (Special Issue), pp. 33–43

McGurk, P. (2009) 'Developing "middle managers" in the public services: The realities of management and leadership development for public managers', *International Journal of Public Management*, Vol. 22 (6), pp. 464–477

Menzies, J. (2017) 'Meeting in the middle: Building a knowledge partnership between academia and government', *Paper to the IRSPM*, Budapest

Milward, H.B. and Provan, K.G. (2006) *A Manager's Guide to Choosing and Using Collaborative Networks*, Washington, DC: IBM Centre for the Business of Government

Mintzberg, H. (1975) 'The manager's job: Folklore and fact', *Harvard Business Review*, July–August, pp. 49–61

Moore, M.E. (1995) *Creating Public Value: Strategic Management in Government*, Cambridge, MA: Harvard University Press

Morse, R. (2007) 'Developing public leaders in an age of collaborative governance', *Leading the Future of the Public Sector: The Third Transatlantic Dialogue,* Newark, DE: University of Delaware

National Academy of Public Administration (2002) *The 21st Century Federal Manager: A Study of Changing Roles and Competencies*, Washington, DC: National Academy of Public Service

National Academy of Public Administration (2004) *Final Report and Recommendations: The 21st Century Federal Manager*, Washington, DC: National Academy of Public Service

National Academy of Public Administration (2007) *Building a 21st Century SES: Ensuring Leadership Excellence in Our Federal Government*, Washington, DC: National Academy of Public Service

National Academy of Public Administration (2017) *No Time to Wait: Building a Public Service for the 21st Century*, Washington, DC: National Academy of Public Service

Needham, C. and Mangan, C. (2013) *The 21st Century Public Servant*, Birmingham: University of Birmingham

Needham, C., Mangan, C. and Dickinson, H. (2013) *The 21st Century Public Service Workforce: Eight Lessons from the Literature*, Birmingham: University of Birmingham

Nicolini, D., Powell J., Conville, P. and Martinez-Solano, L. (2008) 'Managing knowledge in the healthcare sector: A review', *International Journal of Knowledge Management*, Vol. 10 (3), pp. 245–263

Noble, G. and Jones, R. (2006) 'The role of boundary-spanning managers in the establishment of public-private partnerships', *Public Administration*, Vol. 84 (4), pp. 891–917

Nonaka, I. (1994) 'A dynamic theory of organizational knowledge creation', *Organization Science*, Vol. 5 (1), pp. 15–37

Noordegraaf, M. (2015) *Public Management: Performance, Professionalism and Politics*, London: Palgrave Macmillan

Nooteboom, B. (2008) 'Learning and innovation in inter-organizational relationships', in S. Cropper, M. Ebers, C. Huxham and P. Smith Ring (eds) *The Oxford Handbook of Inter-Organizational Relations,* pp. 607–634, Oxford: Oxford University Press

O'Flynn, J., Blackman, D. and Halligan, J. (2014) *Crossing Boundaries in Public Management and Policy: The International Experience*, London: Routledge

O'Leary, R.M. (2015) 'From silos to networks: Hierarchy to heterarchy', in M.E. Guy and M.M. Rubin (eds) *Public Administration Evolving: From Foundations to the Future*, London: Routledge

O'Leary, R. and Bingham, L.B. (2007) *A Manager's Guide to Resolving Conflicts in Collaborative Networks*, Washington, DC: IBM Centre for the Business of Government

O'Leary, R. and Bingham, L.B. (2009) *The Collaborative Public Manager: New Ideas for the Twenty-First Century*, Washington, DC: Georgetown University Press

O'Leary, R. and Gerard, C. (2012) *Collaboration Across Boundaries: Insights and Tips from Federal Senior Executives*, Washington, DC: IBM Centre for the Business of Government

O'Leary, R., Gerard, C. and Bingham, L.B. (2006) 'Introduction to the symposium on collaborative public management', *Public Administration Review*, Vol. 66 (supplement), pp. 6–9

O'Leary, R., Choi, Y. and Gerard, C.M. (2012) 'The skill set of the successful collaborator', *Public Administration Review*, November/December Special Issue, S70–S83

Oomsels, P. and Bouckaert, G. (2014) 'Studying interorganizational trust in public administration', *Public Performance and Management Review*, Vol. 37 (4), pp. 577–604

OPM (2012) *Guide to Senior Executive Service Qualifications*, New York: US Office of Personnel Management

Osborne, S.P. (2010a) *The New Public Governance? Emerging Perspectives on the Theory and Practice of Public Governance*, London: Routledge

Osborne, S.P. (2010b) 'Introduction. The (new) public governance: A suitable case for treatment?', in Osborne, S.P. (ed.) *The New Public Governance?: Emerging Perspectives on the Theory and Practice of Public Governance*, London: Routledge

Oswick, C. and Robertson, M. (2009) 'Boundary objects reconsidered: From bridges and anchors to barricades and mazes', *Journal of Change Management*, Vol. 9 (2), pp. 179–193

O'Toole, L.J. (1996) 'Rational choice and the public management of interorganizational networks', in D.F. Kettl and H.B. Milward (eds) *The State of Public Management*, Baltimore, MD and London: John Hopkins University Press

O'Toole, L.J. and Meier, K.J. (2010) 'Implementation and managerial networking in the new public governance', in S. Osborne (ed.) *The New Public Governance? Emerging Perspectives on the Theory and Practice of Public Governance*, London: Routledge

O'Toole, L.J., Meier, K.J. and Nicholson-Crotty, S. (2005) 'Managing upwards, downwards and outward: Networking, hierarchical relationships and performance', *Public Management Review*, Vol. 7 (1), pp. 45–68

Palmer, I. and Hardy, C. (2000) *Thinking About Management*, London: Sage

Palus, C.J., Chrobot-Mason, D.L. and Cullen, K.L. (2014) 'Boundary spanning leadership in an interdependent world', in J. Langan-Fox and C.L. Cooper (eds) *Boundary-spanning in Organizations: Network, Influence, and Conflict*, London: Routledge

Parise, S. and Prusak, L. (2006) 'Partnerships for knowledge creation', in L. Prusak and E. Matson (eds) *Knowledge Management and Organizational Learning: A Reader*, pp. 125–135, Oxford: Oxford University Press

Parry, K.W. and Bryman, A. (2006) 'Leadership in organizations', in S.R. Clegg, C. Hardy, T.B. Lawrence and W. Nord (eds) *The Sage Handbook of Organization Studies*, London: Sage

Pawlowsky, P., Forslin, J. and Reinhardt, R. (2001) 'Practices and tools of organizational learning', in M. Dierkes, A. Berthoin Antal, J. Child and I. Nonaka (eds) *Handbook of Organizational Learning and Knowledge*, pp. 775–793, Oxford: Oxford University Press

Pearce, C.L. and Conger, J.A. (2003) *Shared Leadership: Reframing the Hows and Whys of Leadership*, London: Sage

Percy-Smith, J., Burden, T., Darlow, L., Hawtin, M. and Ladi, S. (2003) *Promoting Change through Research: The Impact of Research in Local Government*, York: York Publishing Press

Popp, J.K., Milward, H.B., MacKean, G., Casebeer, A. and Lindstrom, R. (2014) *Inter-Organizational Networks: A Review of the Literature to Inform Practice*, Washington, DC: The IBM Center for the Business of Government

Poxton, R. (1993) *Working Across the Boundaries*, London: King's Fund Publishing

Radin, B. (1996) 'Managing across boundaries', in D.F. Kettl and H.B. Milward (eds) *The State of Public Management*, Baltimore, MD and London: John Hopkins University Press

Radin, B. (2009) 'The instruments of intergovernmental management', in B.G. Peters and J. Pierre (eds) *The Handbook of Public Administration*, London: Sage

Rai, R.J. (2011) 'Knowledge management and organizational culture: A theoretical integrative framework', *Journal of Knowledge Management*, Vol. 15 (5), pp. 779–801

Ranson, S. and Stewart, J. (1994) *Management for the Public Domain: Enabling the Learning Society*, Basingstoke: Macmillan Press

Rashman, L., Withers, E. and Hartley, J. (2009) 'Organizational learning and knowledge in public service organizations: A systematic review of the literature', *International Journal of Management Reviews*, Vol. 11 (4), pp. 463–494

Reeves, S., Pelone, F., Harrison, R., Goldman, J. and Zwarenstein, M. (2017) 'Interprofessional collaboration to improve professional practice and healthcare outcomes', *Cochrane Database of Systematic Reviews*, 2017, Issue 6. Art No. CD 000072. DOI: 10.1002/14651858. CD 000072. pub3.

Ryan, B., Gill, D. and Eppel, E. (2008) 'Managing for Joint Outcomes: Connecting Up the Horizontal and the Vertical', *Policy Quarterly*, Vol. 4, Issue 3, pp. 14-21

Salaman, L.M. (2002) *The Tools of Governance: A Guide to New Governance*, New York: Oxford University Press

Salk, J.E. and Simonin, B.L. (2005) 'Beyond alliances: Towards a meta-theory of collaborative learning', in M. Easterby-Smith and M.A. Lyles (eds) *The Blackwell Handbook of Organizational Learning and Knowledge Management*, pp. 253–277. Oxford: Blackwell

Sandfort, J. and Milward, H.B. (2008) 'Collaborative service provision in the public sector', in S. Cropper, M. Ebers, C. Huxham and P. Smith Ring (eds) *The Oxford Handbook of Inter-Organizational Relations*, Oxford: Oxford University Press

Schein, E.H. (2004) *Organizational Culture and Leadership* (3rd edn), San Francisco, CA: Jossey-Bass

Scott, R. and Boyd, R. (2017) *Interagency Performance Targets: A Case Study of New Zealand's Results Programme*, Washington, DC: IBM Centre for the Business of Government

Seddon, J. (2008) *Systems Thinking in the Public Sector*, Axminster: Triarchy Press

Senge, P. (1990) *The Fifth Discipline*, New York: Doubleday

Silvia, C. and McGuire, M. (2010) 'Leading public sector networks: An empirical examination of integrative leadership behaviors', *Leadership Quarterly*, Vol. 21, pp. 264–277

Simpson Review (2011) *Local, Regional, National: What services are best delivered where?*, Cardiff: Welsh Government

Smith, C. (2013) *Beyond Evidence-Based Policy in Public Health: The Interplay of Ideas*, Basingstoke: Palgrave Macmillan

Snyder, W.M. and de Souza Briggs, X. (2003) *Communities of Practice: A New Tool for Government Managers*, Arlington, VA: IBM Centre for the Business of Government

Soun Jang, H., Valero, J.N. and Jung, K. (2016) *Effective Leadership in Network Collaboration: Lessons Learned from Continuum of Care Homeless Programs*, Washington, DC: IBM Center for the Business of Government

Spreitzer, G. and Quinn, R.E. (1996) 'Empowering middle managers to be transformational leaders', *The Journal of Applied Behavioral Science*, Vol. 32 (3), pp. 237–261

Stacey, R.D. (2010) *Complexity and Organizational Reality*, London: Routledge

Star, S.L. and Griesemer, J.R. (1989), 'Institutional ecology, "translations" and boundary objects: Amateurs and professionals in Berkeley's Museum of Vertebrate Zoology, 1907–39', *Social Studies in Science*, Vol. 19 (3), pp. 387–420

Sullivan, H. and Skelcher, C. (2002) *Working across Boundaries: Collaboration in Public Services*, Basingstoke: Palgrave Macmillan

Sullivan, H. and Williams, P. (2012) 'Whose kettle? Exploring the role of objects in managing and mediating the boundaries of integration of health and social care', *Journal of Organization and Management*, Vol. 26 (6), pp. 697–712

Sullivan, H., Williams, P. and Jeffares, S. (2012a) 'Leadership for collaboration: Situated agency', *Public Management Review*, Vol. 14 (1), pp. 41–66

Sullivan, H., Williams, P.M., Marchington, M. and Knight, L. (2012b) 'Collaborative futures: Discursive realignments in austere times', *Public Money and Management*, Vol. 33 (2), pp. 123–130

Swann, W.L. and Kim, S.Y. (2018) 'Practical prescriptions for governing fragmented governments', *Policy and Politics*, Vol. 46 (2), pp. 273-92

Sydow, J. (1998) 'Understanding the constitution of interorganizational trust', in C. Lane and R. Bachmann (eds) *Trust In and Between Organizations*, pp. 31–63, Oxford: Oxford University Press

Thatcher, D. (2004) 'Interorganizational partnerships as inchoate hierarchies: A case study of the community security initiative', *Administration and Society*, Vol. 36 (1), pp. 91–127

Thomas, R. and Linstead, A. (2002) 'Losing the plot? Middle managers and identity, *Organization*, Vol. 9 (1), pp. 71–93

Thomas, R., Hardy, C. and Sargent, L. (2007) 'Artifacts in interactions: The production and politics of boundary objects', *AIM Research Working Paper Series*, www.managingpeoplebook. com/userimages/aim_management_innovation.pdf

Tinline, G. and Cooper, G. (2016) *The Outstanding Middle Manager: How to be a Healthy, Happy, High-performing Mid-level Manager*, London: Kogan Page

Turnbull James, K. (2011) *Leadership in Context: Lessons from leadership theory and current leadership development practice*, London: The King's Fund

Uhl-Bien, M. and Arena, M. (2018) 'Leadership for organizational adaptability: A theoretical synthesis and integrative framework', *The Leadership Quarterly*, Vol. 29, pp. 89–104

Uhl-Bien, M. and Marion, R. (2009) 'Complexity leadership in bureaucratic forms of organizing: A meso model', *The Leadership Quarterly*, Vol. 20, pp. 631–650

van der Wal, Z. (2017) *The 21st Century Public Manager*, London: Palgrave

van Meerkerk, I. and Edelenbos, J. (2018) *Boundary Spanners in Public Management and Governance: An Interdisciplinary Assessment*, London: Edward Elgar

van Wart, M. (2003) 'Public-sector leadership theory: an assessment', *Public Administrative Review*, Vol. 63 (2), pp. 214–228

Vera, D. and Crossan, M. (2005) 'Organizational learning and knowledge management: Toward and integrative framework', in M. Easterby-Smith and M.A. Lyles (eds) *The Blackwell Handbook of Organizational Learning and Knowledge Management*, pp. 122–141, Oxford: Blackwell

Warmington, P., Daniels, H., Edwards, A., Brown, S., Leadbetter, J., Martin, D. and Middleton, D. (2004) *Interagency Collaboration: A Review of the Literature*, Bath: The Learning in and for Interagency Working Project, University of Bath

Welsh Government (2003) *The Review of Health and Social Care: Report of the Project Team advised by Derek Wanless*, Cardiff: Welsh Government

Welsh Government (2004) *Making the Connections*, Cardiff: Welsh Government

Welsh Government (2010) *Setting the Direction: Primary and Community Services Strategic Delivery Programme*, Cardiff: Welsh Government

Welsh Government (2011) *Sustainable Social Services for Wales: A Framework for Action*, Cardiff: Welsh Government

Welsh Government (2012) *Shared purpose – Shared delivery*, Cardiff: Welsh Government

Welsh Government (2013) *Collaborative Footprint for Wales*, Cardiff: Welsh Government

Welsh Government (2014) *Commission on Public Service Governance and Delivery*, Cardiff: Welsh Government

Wenger, E. (1998) *Communities of Practice: Learning, Meaning, and Identity*, Cambridge: Cambridge University Press

Westley, F.R. (1990) 'Middle managers and strategy: Microdynamics of inclusion', *Strategic Management Journal*, Vol. 11 (5), pp. 337–351

WHO (World Health Organization) (2010) *Framework for Action on Interprofessional Education and Collaborative Practice*, Geneva: Health Professions Network Nursing and Midwifery Office, Human Resources for Health

Williams, P. (2002) 'The competent boundary spanner', *Public Administration*, Vol. 80 (1), pp. 103–124

Williams, P. (2012a) *Collaboration in Public Policy and Practice: The Role of Boundary Spanners*, Bristol: Policy Press

Williams, P.M. (2012b) 'Integration of health and social care: A case of learning and knowledge management, *Health and Social Care in the Community*, Vol. 20 (5), pp. 550–560

Williams, P. (2013a) *Integration in Health and Social Care: The Locality Model and the Design and Delivery of Mental Health Services in Cwm Taf LHB* (unpublished)

Williams, P. (2013b) *Managing in Collaboration: A Local Government Perspective* (unpublished)

Williams, P. (2014) *Working in Partnership: The Police and Crime Commissioners* (unpublished)

Williams, P. (2017) *An Assessment of Middle Mangers' Approaches to Collaboration in South East Wales* (unpublished)

Williams, P. (2018) 'The practical challenge', in G. Carey, H. Dickinson and L. Craven (eds) *Crossing Boundaries in Public Management and Policy: Tackling the Critical Challenges*, London: Palgrave

Williams, P. and Sullivan, H. (2009) 'Faces of integration', *International Journal of Integrated Care*, Vol. 9 (December), pp. 1–13

Woodruffe, C. (1992) 'What is a competency?', in R. Boam (ed.) *Designing and Achieving Competency*, Maidenhead: McGraw-Hill

Yin, R.K. (1989) *Case Study Research: Design and Methods*, London: Sage

Index

6 et al. 34, 35, 113, 135

A

accountability 11, 36, 140–1, 144
 management of 41
 mechanisms of *141*
achievability 67
activation 39, 45
active coordination 39–40
adjustment *44*
administration, management and
 3–4
advocacy 37
age of austerity 2, 62, 63, 65
agencies 36
agency 52–3, 91, 103–4, 126, 196
 and boundary objects 96
Agranoff, R. 46–8, 113, 118, 132,
 135
 on balancing organisational and
 collaborative roles 142
 on the importance of middle
 managers 142–3
Allred et al. 189, 197
analysis *44*
analytical ability *147*
analytical competency *156*
Ansell, C. and Torfing, J. 28–9
appraisal *44*
ARACY Factsheet 46, 153–5, *154*,
 179
architecture *44*
assessment *44*
assignment *44*
attention to detail 37
attributes 27, 42–51, *55*, *154*
 and skills 59
 distinction from 151
auditing frameworks 11
Australian Research Alliance for
 Children and Youth (ARACY)
 122
autonomy 37

B

Balogun, J. 23
Bardach, E. 50–1
bed blocking *87*
Bingham et al. 161
boundaries
 framework 93–4
 perspectives on 92
 properties 92
 reinforcement of 166
boundary-crossing 166–7, *173*
boundary object theory 95, 96,
 101
boundary objects 94
 characteristics of *99*
 description of 95
 effectiveness of 99–100
 representation of 95
 symbolism 97
 transformational 97
 types of 96, *97*
boundary spanners 59, 132, 135,
 136, 189–90
 dual personalities of 114
 experience *150*
 importance of 42
 key roles 43
 skills and competencies 42, 43
 coordinator role 43
 entrepreneurial function 43
 interpreter/communicative
 function 43
 reticulist role 43
 subjective evaluations by 114, 115
 and trust 114–15
 typology of 43
bureausclerosis 183
business schools 194
Business Studies Programmes 162

C

calculative source of trust 116–17
capabilities *173*
capacity building programmes
 177–8

229